Fatherh

Insights, wisdom and advice

from fathers for fathers.

T.C.
Many thanks for
your contributions
to this.
Bill

Bill McCusker

Fatherhood: In Pieces

Forward

I wish I had read this book twenty years ago. It would have helped me be a better father to my kids. And it would have helped my marriage.

I remember bringing our first newborn home from the hospital. Amidst the joy and excitement, my wife and I asked ourselves, with a touch of panic, "Now what do we do?" It quickly became clear that the kid didn't come with an instruction manual. No work plan with tasks, responsibilities, start dates, and time frames.

Over the years, my wife and I tried to be good parents. Along the way, I recalled how my parents handled challenges of all sorts. I thought of how my dad approached his role as a father, and I watched how my brothers, friends and colleagues were handling theirs. As my kids got older, I thought about what parents' priorities should be and what their most important roles were. I increasingly recognized the importance of love, guidance, discipline and sacrifice. The responsibility to "get it right" in shaping the lives of one's children was serious business. Some issues were easy to handle; other less so. I increasingly realized that the cliché about parenting being a tough job is more than a cliché.

For the most part, at least in the beginning, I think my wife and I got more things right than wrong, though at times we were clueless, both as individuals and as a team. Later, we began to struggle. We may have been on the same page early on, but with the onset of the teen years especially, we learned, sadly, that we often were far apart. We seemed to be working from different playbooks, and we found it hard to reconcile our conflicting beliefs and approaches. This book could have helped us better frame some of our disagreements, understand our differences, sort through options, and agree on a way forward on any number of issues.

For years, I toyed with the idea of doing this book. It would be based on one-on-one interviews with a number of fathers: old, young, white, black, blue collar guys and CEOs. Fathers talking about what it means to be a father based on their personal experiences. Older guys looking back, and younger guys closer to the starting line. I would listen to their stories. I figured some might be scarred with a few regrets, while others would be brimming with confidence. They would all have two things in common. First, they would be taking their role as a father very seriously. Second, they would be willing to talk honestly -- about their successes, their failures, and the advice they would offer to other dads.

I would rely on what I had done many times in my professional life: survey a group of people, capture their responses, analyze opinions, report findings, and suggest next steps -- hopefully in a way that provides fresh thinking, fosters discussion, and promotes decision making towards some desirable outcome.

I began with two assumptions. First, that I could capture a lot of valuable nuggets from these discussions. In my mind, I was correct in this assumption beyond all doubt. The fathers with whom I spoke gave me a ton of valuable insight, perspectives and advice. For a group that is known for not saying much, these guys opened up and bared their souls. The second assumption was that I'd be able to convey the collective wisdom from these discussions in a way that would serve others. You, the reader, will decide if this assumption was valid.

Process. I spoke with thirty-four fathers. Though I heard some similar messages, no two interviews were the same. Many guys laughed. Some cried. I started by asking them to talk about their own fathers. Some described their dads in the most endearing of terms: my best friend, the person in this world I love the most, the guy I hope to become. Some never had fathers. A few said their dads were awful, exactly the opposite of what they wanted to be themselves. One thing became clear quickly: for better or worse, fathers make enormous and lasting impressions on their kids. Knowing this, even if you read no further, here are the first pieces of fatherly advice: decide what kind of father you want to be. Decide what kinds of people you want your kids to become. And decide what you want your kids to say about you when some guy is interviewing them in twenty years.

Organization of this book. For the time-challenged or the attention-deficit disordered, I've made your task easy. This book is a collection of verbatim comments, with minor editing, taken from my thirty-four interviews. I have organized these "pieces" roughly according to the table of contents that follows. Each piece stands alone and is easily digestible. Start wherever you'd like. I list a few questions for your consideration after each section.

What About Mothers? I started this book with an eye on the advice of fathers for other fathers. That remains the main focus. But the deeper I got into the project, the more I realized that this book should also be of interest to:

Mothers. Much of the advice here will serve any parent. More than this, mothers might use this book to form their own opinions and expectations of what their husbands should do to become good fathers to their kids, as well as what roles they themselves should play as good moms.

Couples. This book invites readers to think about where they are now as parents and consider what they might want to do differently. It should promote a deeper conversation between mothers and fathers about how to raise their kids, what they want their kids to become, what roles they will play as parents, how to work together as a team, and many other issues of critical importance.

Sons. Boys can use this book to consider how to be good fathers when it's their turn to give it a try. Further, it might help sons give their dads a better understanding of what it means to be a good father, as well as to articulate what the needs are that they have of their dads.

Daughters. Similarly, girls might use this to help their fathers understand what they need to do to succeed in a vitally important role. Moreover, it would be wonderful, if indeed it's true that girls tend to marry guys who resemble their fathers, if girls could use this book to help shape their choice of a partner who will be a good husband to them and a good father to their kids.

Whoever you are, I hope this book provides useful insight and helpful advice.

What this book isn't. It's not a scientific study. It's not statistically valid research. It's not proven best practices. It's not a cookbook on how to raise high-achieving kids. It's not something the social scientists will salute as academically rigorous. It's not a guide on how to compete with overly-neurotic parents. Frankly, it's a lot less than all this. And hopefully more.

*   *   *

Dedication

To my daughters, Kelly and Mary, with all my love.

To my Dad. May I be half the man you were.

Fatherhood: In Pieces

Contents

Acknowledgements

For the thirty-four fathers I interviewed:

Thank you for your time, candor, and perspectives.

I've often thought about how fortunate your kids are to have you as their fathers.

I wish all fathers, current and prospective, could sit with you and learn what you taught me.

I wish all mothers had a husband as caring as you.

I wish all kids had such a terrific father and such a positive influence in their lives.

For my wife, Tracye:

Thank you for your assistance, encouragement and support.

For my transcriptionist, Stephanie Hampton:

Thank you for your patience, professionalism and good humor.

Describe Your Father

I'm almost just getting to know my dad even though he died a long time ago.

I think every child instinctively knows that they need to have a strong male figure in their life, and when they don't have that, there's a void.

But he wasn't a hugger. He wasn't demonstrative. I know he loved me, but he never showed it.

I went to the funeral of a close friend. His daughter said, "My dad wasn't perfect, but he was perfect for me."

He was extremely bright. Graduated college when he was 19. Finished Wharton in 2½ years. My grandfather was also very successful, at first. He was a money broker who lost everything in the depression and lived the rest of his life as a broken man with no money, so the three boys had to fend for themselves. My dad being the oldest was forced to work well before anybody expected, starting in junior high school. He worked his way through college shoveling coal and hustling pool. He had a photographic memory. Did not have much of a personality. He never knew really how to relate to people. For example, he didn't know what to do when he saw a child. Do you shake its hand, do you pat it on the head, do you kiss it, or you just wave at it? He didn't know what to do with a child, including his own.

*   *   *

My father tried to teach me, and I fought very unsuccessfully to understand, that I had a responsibility to society. My father used to give away a fair amount of money. I used to think he was crazy. I mean, why would you give it away when we could use it? But apparently he did train me. I just didn't realize it. Some of the things we learn from our parents come out years later.

*   *   *

I was an only child. I had a half sister I never knew about until I was an adult. I didn't see my father from when I was an infant until I was 24. There was bad blood between my father and his in-laws. At the time he didn't have much money, didn't have a job, and had just gotten out of the Navy. He had come back to Philadelphia. Things didn't work out and so he moved back to Michigan where he had grown up. And that's where he made his life.

I caught up with him when I was 24. Saw him two or three times a year from then on. It was a little weird when I first met him. It certainly wasn't your typical father-son relationship. But I was with him when he died. We certainly got to be a lot closer. I certainly learned some things from him…had a healthy amount of respect for him.

*   *   *

I didn't have a father growing up but I didn't exactly know what I was missing. Most of the other guys had a father. Growing up, I was a little different for not having a dad but it didn't seem to hold me back a whole lot.

$$* \qquad * \qquad *$$

He's 92 and still practicing law. He's still very lucid. I think prostate cancer is going to get him unfortunately in the not too distant future. But he's a great guy. Way back, he worked for eggs and firewood.

$$* \qquad * \qquad *$$

I think his biggest strength was he wasn't judgmental. He's very good at listening. He might throw out some ideas but he wouldn't necessarily try to solve problems for me. He listened and eventually went, *I'm sure you will figure it out*. He always had good advice if I wanted it, but he was happy to listen and not give advice if I just wanted him to listen. I thought that was a big deal. I'd like it if I could be that way as well.

$$* \qquad * \qquad *$$

He was a big work hard/play hard kind of a guy and had actually been quite successful. The big weakness…he drank too much. I think he also strayed once in a while from his wife.

$$* \qquad * \qquad *$$

I loved my dad. He was my best friend. I miss him every day. And I think he did a phenomenal job instilling certain things in me. A great deal of what I am is based on the way he raised me. I think I'm taking his lessons, values, and processes of raising children, and I hope that I'm bringing them to a level that he would be proud of.

$$* \qquad * \qquad *$$

My dad is a heart break of a man who at a very early age lost his health to tuberculosis. He was often in the hospital when I was growing up. He was an alcoholic for a while; always in very poor health. My mother would deal with five kids while she was working two or three jobs. It was just very, very, very difficult. He was not a happy drunk. He could be mean.

As he got older, he got a lot smarter, though he still smoked two packs of Lucky Strikes a day with one lung, if you can imagine that. He went on to write a column for the local newspaper. Became a city councilman; has a park and a hospital wing named after him in my home town. He was incredibly bright and an orator of very substantial talent, as he showed many times during funeral orations. The guy had a sixth grade education. So I'm very proud of what he accomplished. Not terribly proud of the way he handled raising kids, but I'm not sure I would have fared any better had I been dealt the same cards. He didn't know my kids because he passed away before I had them.

*   *   *

I watched him very closely. I figured out from watching what he did what I didn't want to do. And that was kind of easy.

*   *   *

My dad was diagnosed with a disease called Retinitis Pigmentosa back when he was in his 30s. He hid this from us kids for a long time but he had to retire early. My mom told me this. He worked out a deal with General Electric after he was diagnosed. At the time, they were desperate for people with his qualifications. We were in the space race with the Russians. The Cold War was very hot at that time. They needed people like him who could design rockets and satellites and warheads. He never has talked about the military stuff that he worked on, but I know that he worked on some of those projects.

12

At any rate, he struck a deal with GE where he could retire in his 50s with full pension. But in the mean time, he had to work really hard. And he was always extremely concerned that somehow he was going to lose his job and we were going to be up shit's creek. It actually was only a year or two before my dad retired that I learned that he had this illness. Even though he was rapidly going completely blind, he hid it very well. I should have woken up early to the clues. He was always banging into things, tripping. It was my mom who finally told me what was going on with him.

I never talked to him about why he hid it. But I think it was because he had too much else on his mind. He was too concentrated on supporting us financially to bring us into his circle of confidence. Why did we need to worry about that? That was for him to worry about. So all he did was share his concerns with my mom. Although I do remember when I was 12, my brother was about 16 or 17. He just started to drive and he got into a horrendous car accident and the other person was killed. My brother was hurt but not seriously. And they took him to an eye doctor and that's when they found out my brother has this same disease. My dad just collapsed. I was shocked because I'd never seen him do this before. He was bawling like a baby. I mean, he was devastated to think that this thing that had almost ruined his life was affecting his kids, too.

*   *   *

He was a man of honesty and courage. Deeply religious and very involved with the Church. Never said a bad word about anyone. One of sayings was, *If you can't say something nice about someone, say nothing.* He was also very charitable. He constantly received solicitations from overseas missions, most of which he contributed to. He often said that we need to *Help the least of our brethren.*

*   *   *

13

What could my dad have done better? I'd have to say considering the circumstances, I wish he had been a little more open about what he was going through, but that just wasn't his makeup. I mean, his generation, that wasn't the thing they did. They didn't talk about their problems with their kids. They didn't talk about their problems with anybody really.

*   *   *

He was kind of a distant dad when we were growing up. On weekends, he didn't seek me out to do things with me. He was busy doing his own stuff. That's fine. Everybody needs some time off.

He did a lot of work around the yard which he really enjoyed. He'd sneak off behind the house and smoke his pipe. He thought he was hiding it from all of us but you could smell it.

*   *   *

I was a typical teenager and I rebelled against everything and everybody. We had some difficult moments where I challenged him as the head of the household. I remember telling him at one point, *I don't want to be here anymore,* and he said, *Well, fine. Then get the hell out.* And I did. I left for a few days. I was staying with friends. I remember my mom was calling around frantically trying to find out where I was. She got a hold of my friend's parents and they cornered me. They said, *You have to call home. You can't stay here any longer.* So I did and I talked to my dad and it was one of the first times that we really had a heart to heart. We both ended up apologizing for our behavior and it kind of changed our relationship. I think it was the first time he started to look at me as something more than just a kid. And I saw him as something more than just this remote authoritarian figure.

*   *   *

One thing about my dad that I always tried to copy is his complete devotion to his wife. His love for my mom is just epic in everything that he does. And I try to do that with my kids too. He puts her on a pedestal and she deserves it. She worked hard. She's a great lady, my mom.

*   *   *

My father's influence? I never felt much influence from my father. Why is that? He worked hard; was out of the house most of the nights working. He had to reeducate himself twice with degrees in order to get into different careers because each career didn't work out. So my reflection on him is he seemed to work very, very hard, but he never really imparted a lot of advice to me as a kid. My mother was more dominant. He was a loving father but I don't recall any real messages he delivered other than hard work is a road to success and never be afraid to alter your career path if it's not working out. He used to be a ceramic engineer. He became an accountant, taught himself computers, and became a computer consultant.

*   *   *

He was a great guy. Injured in the war but I didn't hear about it until later. I knew that he was missing a finger. He was in the Battle of the Bulge. Came back home. I don't know if he was a genius or not, but when nobody else was doing computers, he was coming home with tab runs and had to find bugs in computers.

But it turns out that he was battling depression. Was on Prozac and some stuff I became aware of while he was still alive. But for the last five years of his life, he'd sit at home and say, *Golden years, my ass. This sucks.* Never said he wanted to die but if I came home one day and found out that my father committed suicide, it wouldn't have shocked me. However, straight guy. He was one of ten kids. His phrase was always, *Do the right thing.* Every day. After school, after work. Whenever I was around, he'd say, *Hey, always do the right thing.*

*   *   *

Now my mother, we used to call her *the warden* because she was a tough SOB. Great lady and great relationship. But she was the disciplinarian and he was the good guy. That's how a lot of houses were back then. People had to work all those hours. Back then, my father was offered promotions which he turned down because it might mean he'd have to travel, and he was afraid of planes. I always respected his intellect, but I was always disappointed. He could have achieved so much more.

*   *   *

He died at 68 of lung cancer. Smoked four packs a day and was on oxygen for the last year. He was one of ten kids. My mother was one of seven or eight. We moved from the city to Rosalyn, Pennsylvania, and were the first family on either side that moved to the suburbs. As if being in Rosalyn was like being in East Hampton. So by most people's measure, he was probably the most successful of the 17 of them. But I never would have known that because I was used to whatever it was that we had.

*   *   *

He was much younger than his youngest sister. So he was almost like an only child. The first to go to college. He became a physician, and then, when he was about 27, had a Down Syndrome child at a time when people were just starting to think about bringing those individuals back into the home as totally dependent for life. So I reflect a lot on what it would be like to be a father, to be 27, to have a Down Syndrome child, when you didn't have very much means and you didn't have much of a support structure.

*   *   *

My relationship with my father is now and always has been very good. He and my mother both say that we think a lot alike and we probably are more kindred spirits than my other siblings are in terms of thinking alike. Growing up he was a great father. I mean both my parents were great parents so I was fortunate from that perspective. He never forced me into anything but was always supportive of anything that I did no matter what I wanted to do.

He and my mom worked well together. There were not many disagreements they had in front of us. They let us make mistakes on our own but were always supportive and there to help out whenever needed. And even to this day, when I have any issues or questions, I really trust his judgment and will talk to him about almost anything. I often tell him he's never wrong, and he laughs at that. He says to just give him time. But he has very good judgment. As I said, we think a lot alike so maybe that makes it a little bit easier.

*   *   *

I've met many, many people that have worked with my dad in different contexts. They all tell me what a phenomenal guy he is. He really goes out of his way to help other people. He's a pathologist, which can be hard because sometimes he knows bad news about people before they know. He always keeps it very private, but then he'll always do something to try to assist them in whatever ways they need help, and not just in a medical way. He's very humble and understated. You know his big mid-life crisis was to buy himself a Honda Prelude. I wanted him to buy himself a BMW, but he loves his Honda Prelude and he's had it for 15 years.

*   *   *

He's very much an optimist. Almost to the point that I think

17

it's a negative attribute. <u>Everything</u> is good. Occasionally I would hear him say some things about my Down Syndrome brother, but he'll always say, *But other people have it worse*. In general, everything is positive. He always encouraged me to do whatever I want to do and not to feel that I had any sort of limitations.

*　　*　　*

One of the things I felt was missing in our relationship, and I'm almost hesitant to say that there's anything missing, but I think he had difficulty connecting on an emotional level. He provided the financial support. If something needed to get done or fixed, he would be there to physically do it or help do it. But I think he had a hard time connecting when it was more emotional. That was more a role my mom played with me.

*　　*　　*

I think I am more comfortable in the area of gray and he is more black and white. He's always there to support me, but it's a very passive support. He doesn't want to direct me. He doesn't want to say, *You should do X* or, *I would do Y*. He wants me to know that he's there with whatever I want to do. I think there were some cases when I was looking for more direction. His father was older when he was growing up, and maybe he didn't have a whole lot of direction and maybe he thought that was a liberating thing. Maybe he thinks that you get to the best answer by finding your own way.

*　　*　　*

I'm almost just getting to know my dad even though he died a long time ago. I can look back now as an adult, father, and a grandfather and see the parts of my dad that I didn't know I had. I don't know that I felt particularly close to him growing up. Certainly not estranged, but I wasn't a buddy in any way. I knew

18

he was there as a protector. Physically strong guy. He just came across that way. Not particularly nurturing but not distant either. In some ways, he was quiet, reserved and distant but not afraid to hug me, kiss me. I didn't feel like I got a lot of guidance from him.

But now I look back and I think of who he was and I believe he provided some pretty good guidance. Incredibly principled human being. My brother and I rode our bikes to get our hair cut for fifty cents or whatever it was back in those days. There was a soda machine there. An extra soda came out and my brother took it home and drank it and somehow my dad found out. My dad made my brother ride his bike back and put another quarter in the machine or give a quarter to the barbershop owner. Just that kind of thing sticks with me that my dad taught me. He taught me integrity to an extreme.

*　　　*　　　*

He was very creative. He had literally hundreds of inventions; one patent but hundreds of little drawing and inventions. Like in the early 1950s, he invented an electric toothbrush but didn't know what to do with it. He'd see a need and create something. I thought that was part of our dad. That's who he was. We didn't think much of it. I think he really taught me to be innovative. To challenge the given. He wrote, and I like to write. I'm sure I got that from him. I think he was somewhat of a rebel. Kind of a quiet rebel that didn't really live out his rebellious feelings. Some ways he did.

He quit school in 8th grade. He was 11th of 12 kids. The youngest boy. Hitchhiked across the country when he was 15 or 16 back in the 1930s. Went to World War II. I always felt like there was a piece of my father that I never got to know because he was in the war. He was on the front lines. Never talked about it. Got injured. Barely talked about that. My mom told me he was in a foxhole with two others, and both his buddies died. My dad ended up with shrapnel in his face and lost some of his hearing. But I lost something too. It's something emotional I must have lost. I didn't know what he was like before the war. How could I? It's just an intuitive sense. So what I learned from him is to hate war even though he would never have said that. He was a very strong patriot. Not that I'm not, but it was intense as a kid growing up. I really respected the people that fought in Vietnam, but my dad didn't like the war at all. I was just a teenager. And yet, every Veterans Day I call my friends who are veterans and thank them. My dad never taught me that directly.

*   *   *

He was very respectful of women. You couldn't tell a dirty joke or anything that came close to a dirty joke in front of my dad, but when he wasn't there, my mom would tell us dirty jokes. I think he was very much a gentleman. He didn't drink. I guess a beer here and there. But apparently when he was young, came back from the war, he drank pretty good. Had his first heart attack on his anniversary when he was 48. I was at my little league baseball game when mom came to get me and said my dad had a heart attack. He ended up dying with his fourth or fifth heart attack when he was 65.

*   *   *

From my own growth and my acceptance of who I am, I am able to accept him. I accept why he was the way he was, why he did the things he did, positive and negative. I was always embarrassed that my father only had an eighth grade education and drove a truck for the city of Miami Beach. After he had a second heart attack, they put him on a bridge and he sat there all night long and opened the bridge once an hour. This bright and creative guy going nuts. I was embarrassed to tell my friends that. Most of my friends' parents were professional people. I was always embarrassed when people would come over my house. It's a perfectly fine house. I didn't want people to know what my dad did, and it took me a long time to get over that.

But I since have accepted who I am and where I come from. He was a pretty amazing guy. The principle side of me, which is pretty strong, all comes from him and I'm proud of that. I'm proud of my integrity. I'm proud of my efforts. He didn't accomplish much in the way that most people see accomplishment, but I now feel I was a pretty good accomplishment. I never felt like that. I was never that confident. But now I recognize that by accepting myself, I am accepting my dad completely. And I couldn't do that when I was 29 years old. I regret that my dad doesn't know how much I appreciated what he did for me.

*   *   *

He was a very committed father who took his responsibilities to provide for the family very seriously. That was his number one priority. To make enough money so that we always had good food on the table and clothes to wear. We lived as well as we could. He was not extravagant at all. Very, very frugal as a matter of fact but we never wanted for any of life's necessities.

*   *   *

He was not the type of dad who was involved in your daily life. His job was to go to work, make the money, come home and be the disciplinarian when necessary. But it wasn't like he'd go to ballgames and watch us do things and be active. Kind of what's expected of me today. But you know, he was always there when it was important. He was certainly there when we were out of line.

*   *   *

About certain things, he was very strict and he had no problem with corporal punishment, so I got lots of spankings. I

21

probably deserved half of them at least. But, he was a good dad. I got no complaints. Would it have been nice if he taken more interest in things? Yeah, but you know, it's also tough to make a living. You come home. You're tired. Sometimes you're working two jobs. I never felt that I was missing anything.

*   *   *

Some of the attributes that I would ascribe to him? Frugal would be one. Hardworking would be one. Committed would be one. A Chinese immigrant, a lot of the aspects of his Chinese upbringing followed him everywhere. Things like respect. Respect for your elders was huge. Even to this day, my mother still somehow takes care of older relatives. That was a big thing with him: respect for your elders. Respect for authority was huge. You didn't break the rules. You didn't break the law. You didn't want to make trouble. Don't step out of line. Don't draw attention to yourself that way.

*   *   *

He's 75. It's interesting, as he got older and his kids matured, I believe he matured more. He mellowed out quite a bit. He had a temper when I was young. But I could see him mellowing out as we got older. Actually, especially around his grandchildren, he doted on his grandchildren far more than I ever remember him doting on us.

I think it's a learning that everybody goes through. Because when I look back at my parents, I think they made a lot of mistakes in raising the earlier siblings. I got the benefit of them having learned from their earlier trials. I think they made some major, major mistakes in how they raised the older kids.

*   *   *

I didn't know my father. My parents were divorced so I was one of those kids who grew up without a father. He was introduced into my life when I was around 12 or 13 years old. By then, I guess you already formulated a lot of your own personality and perspective. Fortunately or unfortunately, I had developed a perspective that whatever I did, I was going to do something different. I would never be the kind of father who wouldn't play a prominent role in my children's lives.

*   *   *

I think every child instinctively knows that they need to have a strong male figure in their life, and when they don't have that, there's a void. An emptiness. I probably didn't even realize it at the time when I was growing up, but now looking back on it, I can say that there was something missing. I know it because as I got older, I met men who mentored me and behaved in a fatherly way toward me. There was a sense of fulfillment that I experienced in those relationships that I didn't realize was missing until I had those experiences.

But once I did meet him and got to know him, there were certain things about him that I liked and understood and appreciated. And other things that I was just happy to say, *I'm glad I'm not like that guy.*

*   *   *

Maybe my dad was selfish about certain things that he had in his life. He put boundaries around his things that he wanted to do. So, I think I'm better incorporating my son into those things that I have interests in. I'm not so sure my dad was as good as incorporating me into his.

*   *   *

23

My father was tenacious. He could get anything done. I picked him up to play golf when he was 89 years old. Hadn't seen him for a couple of months. I asked, *Dad, how you doing?* He said, *I'm so busy!* And he was. He was a great organizer. Always had projects. He was like a dog on a bone. He would execute the hell out of anything that he took on. Church stuff. Charities. Golf trips. He never stopped.

*   *   *

His own father died when he was 12. So he didn't have much of a role model himself but he worked his way through. He loved athletics, for example, but could never really participate because he always had to work after school. And he worked his way through college even in the Depression. But he always made it very clear that he had two priorities for his children. One was their health and the other was their education. He just figured that if he could give his four kids the best education that he could afford, then it would be up to them to figure out what they could do with it.

*   *   *

I went to the funeral of a close friend. His daughter said, *My dad wasn't perfect, but he was perfect for me.*

*   *   *

It's funny how he had some expressions that he used that I still use today. One is, *You can't put an old head on young shoulders.* What he meant is that you can't expect a young person to have the wherewithal to make the kinds of decisions or judgments that someone with years of experience would. If they make bad choices, it's because they don't know otherwise, so don't make them feel guilty. Don't hold them irrevocably responsible for the fact that they can't make decisions beyond the scope of their own age and experience. He didn't make us feel as though there

24

was something wrong with us because we made a choice that was the result of our youth. It's a great expression.

*   *   *

He was of the generation of men where it was very hard for him to express his love. But he did. I still think of him all the time. I remember one time when I was teaching. I was about 25 years old and it had been a very hard year academically. And I just needed to get out of Dodge. I needed to get off on my own and just decompress. So I got in the car in Philadelphia and I drove north to Mount Washington up in the White Mountains. Got there way too late in the afternoon. But I got on the trail and I climbed straight up Mount Washington to the Lake of the Clouds hut where you can spend the night. I got there at like 9 at night. It was pitch black. Thank God they had a bunk so I could spend the night.

So the next day I climbed up to a place at the top where they measure wind speed. And there's a telephone. I thought I ought to call my dad and surprise him. So I called him from the top of Mount Washington. Now they lived in Cleveland. He had no idea where I was or what I was doing. I said, *I'll bet you can't guess where I am.* He said, *I'll bet you're in the White Mountains.* Out of the blue. It was a recognition that he knew me better than I thought. How did he ever figure that out? It seems like a silly story but I just remember how shocked I was that he could possibly have a clue. Now I had gone to camp up in that area when I was 13, 14 and 15. Maybe he remembered how much I liked it. But it shocked me that he was that knowledgeable about me.

*   *   *

As his son, he saw in me a blend of academic interest and athletic interest which he had. He wanted people to be healthy and he thought athletics were a key part of that. He exercised all the way up to the day he died. I think he weighed within one pound of the weight he was when he graduated from college.

*   *   *

You know, it's funny how my father died 18 years ago and I still can't talk about him without crying. I don't know how I gave the eulogy for both of my parents. Five hundred people attended my father's funeral. I don't quite know how I got through that. But I felt I owed it to him and had to do him the honor. I didn't know how I was going to do it. I had to practice about 30 times. I'd do it in front of the mirror. I'd do it in front of my own mother because I knew she would cry. So I had to do it and see her and not cry myself.

*   *   *

I was the eighth of eight kids so I think by the time I came around, he was kind of that dad who you saw but you never really spent time with. He was working constantly. We grew up in a three bedroom, one bath home with eight kids. You can quickly figure out it was tough going. He was a mortgage broker and loved being able to keep my mom home. But he overly relied on my mother to take care of all the family stuff. He'd come home, have a couple of beers, and he'd say hello to you and that was it.

And as I got older and as I got more involved in athletics, that's when the two us really started to bond. He would make every single football game. And then from a basketball perspective, I was playing in three summer leagues every year, and some nights I had three games. And he would zip me to and from every one of those games. Never missed a game. The amazing part of that is, when I was in 7th grade, I was the worst basketball player on the team. When I was in 8th grade I was the tallest and worst player, and I didn't even get off the bench.

But he went to every game and was there for me even

though I never played. I always joked with my buddies that I couldn't walk and chew gum. I just wasn't coordinated back then, but he was there all the time. He played high school basketball and tried to go to college, but my father just couldn't afford it. He was almost at every practice. When I went to college, I think that was one of the proudest moments of his life. I started my freshman year and he would sit in the same spot every game which was basically the same section that he sat in in high school.

*   *   *

His greatest weakness? Had it not been for basketball or football with me, I think I wouldn't have had a relationship with him. I look at some of my siblings who didn't have the basketball or football that I had. They didn't have much of a relationship with him. And I think in his mind set, he brought home money and that was his job. And if he wasn't doing his job, he was hanging out at the Knights of Columbus bar in Springfield and would drink and then come home and just go to sleep. During the summer, he'd bring us to the pool. We'd be swimming all day. He'd stay in the bar the whole day. Then he'd throw us all in the car and we'd drive home. I think that was his biggest weakness. He never understood the power that a father can have as an influence on his children. He's not a bad person. That's just who he is.

*   *   *

I think he was an alcoholic. He never went to AA or anything like that. He's had congestive heart failure about 10 times in the last year and a half, all because of his drinking. And he just won't stop. My siblings and I say one of these times he's going to drink himself to death.

I rarely drink in front of the kids. And I never have beer in the house. Never. I have an outside refrigerator in the garage, and the kids basically don't even know it's there and that's where I keep my beer. But I never like to drink in front of them. Although if I'm cooking out on the grill, I will grab a beer but I don't keep it in the bottle. I put it in a mug. That's just the way I am.

*   *   *

My father's biggest strength was providing for the family. You could feel his love, but he never expressed it. You could sense his pride for his kids, mainly for me, but you'd never really felt it directly.

*   *   *

He passed away 10 years ago. I thought that he was really a great guy. Probably middle class. Was better at enjoying life than I think I am. Had a great group of friends and colleagues and was very family oriented, very responsible. My dad was one of 10 kids. He was the one who stayed in touch with all nine brothers and sisters much better than anyone else. Very family oriented. High sense of responsibility. You took care of your family, you took care of your responsibilities. But he enjoyed life. Was a good advocate when he needed to be. Had a strength about him. Many times I think to myself, what would my dad have done in this circumstance? Especially when it comes to family or just living. Not much in business. My career is quite different than his career was.

*   *   *

I think we were always close. Even as a kid I don't ever remember having trouble talking to him. There were certainly things you didn't talk to your parents about, like drugs and alcohol. But other than that, I don't ever remember having a tough time talking to my dad. As I got older, I talked to him about a lot more serious kinds of stuff. I miss not having him available to talk to. I miss not having him to pal around with. We went to ballgames

28

when I was a kid, and I can remember when I was older it was still a lot of fun to go to games with him. I can remember the opening day game for the Detroit Tigers. Freezing cold, snow on the ground. It was cool being able to go to the opener. My dad let me skip school on opening day. I can remember going with him on the weekends to visit relatives. The family would talk and just sit there laughing it up. He was a great guy. I couldn't have asked for a better father. I really, really enjoyed it.

*   *   *

He worked all the time. He brought work home every night. He traveled. He worked on weekends. He always had the briefcase open. He'd be with us but he was always in his work. But at the same time, all the kids loved him. I mean all my friends and the nieces and nephews all loved him. If it was a holiday, and all the parents would be inside cooking and talking, he'd always be out playing football with the kids or cheating at basketball, stepping on people's toes, pulling their pants because he couldn't jump as high as them. He was just a kid at heart and still is.

*   *   *

He was always very supportive of whatever I did. He expected me not to quit. To work hard at whatever I did. If I decided not to do something or do something, as long as there was some value to it, he and my mom were supportive of it and would help us wherever they could. I think a lot of my style was influenced by my dad. My wife always says, *You're frighteningly similar*, and that's a compliment to both of us.

*   *   *

Army basic training was the first time that I met strong men. And I was fascinated with the whole area of leadership. And I became a sergeant very quickly and I think it made all the difference in my life. It filled the absence of not having a dad.

*   *   *

My father was a Philadelphia police officer, and at that time they rotated shifts. I don't think they still do that. They start with 12 to 8 and then 8 to 4. And I never remember having a family meal. Not one. I can't remember a lot of things about my dad that were pleasant or helpful.

*   *   *

My dad's biggest strengths are that he is affable, he's pleasant, he's never had a bad word to say, he never had a bad day that I can remember. He's never been inappropriate, never been drunk, never been yelling at my mother, never…he's just been a superstar my whole life. To ask, what were his weaknesses? I can't think of any.

*   *   *

He had an old Buick and he always had a cigar in his mouth. And when we'd get in the car, he would bite off the end of the cigar and spit it out. Some pieces stuck on the windshield, others dropped onto the dashboard. That's one of the few things I remember. I never had a lot of time with him. No family interaction.

*   *   *

He was a passive participant in life. He was the observer. We didn't do a lot. What I've learned, what I want to do different, is to be active, very active in my kids' stuff. Coaching, baseball, soccer or going on their scouting trips. He'd talk; he was the guy who was never at a loss for words. But the conversation was a monologue. It was not a conversation. So I guess the other thing is

I tend to listen more than I talk. I got that from him. You know, not wanting to replicate what I saw. Just smell the roses, enjoy my kids. Not that he didn't enjoy us, it was just a passive involvement versus an active one.

*   *   *

My dad had a 1967 Pontiac Lamont. His first car with air-conditioning. And we drove from Ohio to Colorado and he smoked the whole way there. He never rolled down the windows because it would "break the seal" or something. So we drove two days straight, my dad chain-smoking in the front seat. I sat in the back seat with a pillow over my face. I don't know how old I was at the time. I would never smoke because of that.

*   *   *

Life goes so fast and I want to enjoy it and appreciate it. I don't want to be in my dad's situation 40 years from now where I don't have any link to my kids. I want to stay relevant with my kids and build that bridge. You have to build it now because there's no guarantee that you can later on. My dad and I didn't build that bridge when I was young. It's hard to build it now.

*   *   *

My father had a tremendous sense of humor and a very high thirst for knowledge and would challenge us on a number of things. He was known as a trivia king and he called himself *The Iron Duke*. Start a topic, start a phrase, and he would have an answer. Probably nine out of ten times he was bullshitting us, but with such confidence that it wasn't until we were older that we realized that he would have given an answer to anything. Sometimes he was right. He would have been interesting to be on *Jeopardy*. At least he would never be short of an opinion or an answer even if he had no clue what he was talking about.

31

*   *   *

He was on the cover of a magazine, a guy with his toys, all of his paraphernalia. He was the president of the Valley Forge Signal Seekers which is a radio controlled verifier. You drive into the park on a Saturday or Sunday and they're flying these little planes. He was the president. After he retired, he became part of a national air show team that went around with miniature Thunderbirds to Kenosha, Wisconsin, Maguire Air force Base, and Willow Grove. He was part of the show team. He had a gold jumpsuit with his name on the back. He was a kid all the way to the end. I think that's a healthy perspective that I appreciated. You need to have fun. You need to stay young because if you don't, you just grow up. He loved games, he loved cards, his toys. He also was an engineer.

He played with air conditioning. I mean there wasn't anything he couldn't have built from scratch or without a plan. So very handy. The irony is, here's a guy who worked in air conditioning his whole life who never had air conditioning until we moved to Philadelphia. It was so hot here. The summer of '64, '65 was one of those heat wave summers. The next summer my mom insisted that we get air conditioning. He said he'll put the air conditioning in, but he'll do it himself. And I'd have to be his apprentice. We worked up in the attic in 100 degree heat. We built the duct work. He had the machines air lifted in. Then he cut the holes in the side of the house where the air conditioner came in. He designed the whole thing. He did all the electrical work, all the plumbing, all the duct work in a four bedroom house with a 14 year old assistant who couldn't say no.

*   *   *

I did not have a close relationship with my father. My father was a very smart man and very successful, but he was also a violent alcoholic. That made me very tough because I never allowed myself to become a victim. I rejected that. And so there are certain rules that I put on myself. For instance, I would never drink alone. I drink, but I would never have a drink on my own. There has to be a reason to have a drink, say with someone socially or a glass of wine with dinner with my wife. There are certain rules that I have in place. I'm much more self disciplined than my father was. I would never allow myself to get into certain situations because I saw what he did to himself. He died very young.

My brothers and I are much stronger people than our father. You know, like alcohol, we totally rejected that. And the violence and everything else. I had a shocking relationship with my father because I would not give in to him, and I fought him even from a very young age. Dad would lay into me. I'd fight back. I never became a victim to his weaknesses. I had no hang-ups about that. He was a dickhead. You know, what can I say. It was a stupid thing to do to allow himself to become an alcoholic and behave that way. I have no respect for that, but I don't have any hang-ups about it. That was his choice and it hasn't affected my life. I have rejected so much of what he did. So I learned a great deal from my dad about what not to do.

*   *   *

My father was clearly an authoritative figure in our house but he was also a very warm and gentle guy. And that warmth and gentleness impressed me and it certainly allowed me to be close to him. The time that we did have with him was good stuff. It was quality time. I don't know where the hell he got this from because his father passed away when he was young. I don't think he got this from his father. When my nieces and nephews were growing up and he was still around, he would do this thing with each of the grandkids, which was fascinating. Each of the grandkids still remembers this. He would get together with them at different holidays and say, *Come on, sit down, and I'll read your bumps.* And the kids were anywhere from three to seven years old and my father would be gently massaging their scalp. He'd just be talking about different things he could recognize in them. These kids were totally locked in on that. And they looked forward, when it was gatherings with the family and grandpa was going to be there, to having their bumps read by grandpa.

*   *   *

I want to be like my father in some areas, and there are other areas where I want to be different. My father was first generation. His parents both came over from Italy. He was the oldest boy and the second oldest child. After high school, he pretty much went to work to help support the family. There were six kids, so he never had an opportunity to go to college. He was an electrical engineer, worked in aerospace putting in circuit boards. He ended up working for people that were younger than him and had college degrees, so it was very clear to my two brothers and me, from an early age we were going to college. There was never even a question that we were going to go to college. And so from that perspective clearly he was an influence. He always was very stable, very reliable, always there.

Because of his job he didn't travel. He really didn't work a lot of overtime so we had dinner every night pretty much at the same time. He encouraged us to get responsible early on. We had paper routes and after school jobs and things like that. We had certain things we had to do chore wise, but not very much. He just was a very good, kind, and decent person. In fact, people say, *How did you turn out to be such a jerk? Your father was such a nice guy*. He was just a nice guy.

*   *   *

His name was Attilio but they called him Al because nobody would pronounce Attilio. Uncle Al. He was steady and reliable and you always knew what you were going to get with him. He was very honest, high integrity. Never any question of his morals or his character. He didn't drink. He quit smoking when he was young and he realized it was bad for him. At the same time, he was not aggressive. He didn't really try to achieve a lot in his career. He didn't try to expand. I guess he was content to kind of make a good living so he didn't really stretch from that perspective.

*   *   *

Growing up I was probably closer to my mother. Getting in trouble…I was such a smart ass, and then my father got really smart when I went to college. They had a significant influence on me. They, in looking back, did all the right things. He said, *Going out? Have a good time. Remember, you spell your last name the same way I do.* The first time he said that I scratched my head and said, *What's the message in that?* My father was very good at giving messages that weren't assertions. They weren't "don't dos"; they weren't "dos". They were bigger than that. And I think I embraced that. My mom was more "who, what, when, where or why". I was pretty clever, and you can get around the "who, what, when, where and why". Those questions, those interrogations, don't always work. He took the high ground; gave me a bit of a moral compass, if you will. I actually believe that he knew that he couldn't predict what I was going to encounter, so he wanted to give me principles to think about.

*   *   *

My mother was tight and my father was more expansive. And as I learned later on, he was wild. He was more likely to say, *Look, I know what you're doing in high school so just be careful.* There was a looseness in him. You know, drinking. Big issue. My father offered me a drink at home. I was 14 years old. I never saw him under the influence of alcohol. Drinking alcohol was not a big deal to my father. It was, *If you drink, don't embarrass yourself. In*

35

a car, it impairs you. I went to a Catholic school and drinking was a big deal. I actually did not drink in high school. I had a couple of drinks at home. That was it. Because he made it a non big deal.

*   *   *

I was very close with my mother. My father was very distant. He was a guy who struggled with life. Still alive by the way. Struggled with life for many, many years. He's mellowed over time but during the days of growing up, he was an engineer and feared getting fired. He was home every day at 5:15. You know that kind of a dad. He was so wrapped up in worrying. He was a very sad kind of guy. He and I were never close. I got in trouble with him a lot for doing things that I would say were typical kid kinds of things.

I was always a very good athlete. When I came home from college, it might have been Thanksgiving my freshman year, I had friends over. We're throwing the football on my front yard and the ball fell to the ground and rolled toward him. My father picked it up and threw the football very well to my friend. The thing that I remember was not knowing that my father knew how to throw a football. He wasn't the, *Let's go outside and have a catch* kind of dad. And he certainly didn't care at all about the things I was doing. He mostly wanted me to be a better student. Was frequently disappointed because of the typical kid kinds of things that would get me in a lot of trouble. The breaking of a window completely by accident created an unbelievable hailstorm. He was really angry. He was more frustrated. His anger came from frustration. He was corked up; terribly corked up. Probably somewhere between cautious and paranoid. Very cautious guy. So I had a crappy relationship with him unfortunately. Pretty close to my mother still to this day.

*   *   *

36

My dad is my best friend. To this day he's my best friend. He was over yesterday and if I could be half the father to my kids that he is and was to me, I'd be a successful dad. Meaning being their best friend. Them never ever being afraid to come and share anything with me. That's so important to me. To be able to listen to them and not judge them, or give them my feedback if that's what they're after, or say nothing if they just want to be heard. My dad was fantastic with that, and to this day, I'll call him with things. Any problems I may have with my wife or my career, he's the first person I call. My wife's second.

*   *   *

That's how my relationship with my kids differs, in that my dad was not active in entertaining me. He was active in raising me but his agenda was not, *Okay, we're going to go on a picnic and then we're going to go to the library and then we're going to come home and we're going to play football*. It was, *I'm here. I'm your dad. I'm here if you need to talk to me and I'm going to raise you the way I want to raise you. However, go figure it out. Go fall on your face a few times. Go out there and interact. Don't look to me for your entertainment.* It seems like if it were not for us entertaining our kids today, they would just sit. *Okay, I have nothing to do. I have a toy room downstairs and I have computers and things but what else is there to do?* I don't know. I don't know why we do that but we do it. What do I do with my kids? I do a lot. I come home and I'll get them bathed and I'll get them ready for bed and I'll help cook dinner and things like that. My dad never did that. I don't know if that's the Italian in him or not. He never got us dressed or never bathed us, but I love him like no other person on this earth.

*   *   *

My father was a hard-working blue-collar guy whose parents died when he was young. He taught me about respect, about raising kids, and the importance of family. He was street smart and could have a short fuse. He didn't go to college but he was smart. He took pleasure in simple things, like teaching me how to fish.

*   *   *

My dad came from a humble, blue-collar background. He worked hard and was gregarious, playful, and very likeable. He loved people, all people. My father always encouraged me but didn't get in the way. He taught me to be nice to everyone, to respect everyone. For him, it was a blessing just to get up in the morning.

*   *   *

I saw things in my father that I don't want to copy. He was gregarious, had a lot of good people skills, and all my friends liked him. But he wasn't a hugger. He wasn't demonstrative. I know he loved me, but he never showed it.

*   *   *

My father could be emotional and rash. He could be narrow-minded. He was undereducated and he didn't have the processing skills, or wasn't exposed enough to different ways of thinking. As a result, he didn't always draw the right conclusions. My mother was quiet, cerebral and more analytical than my father. I am a combination of both of them, but I tend to be more like her than him.

*   *   *

I never knew him. He was killed in World War II, the same year he got married and the same year I was born. My mother never remarried, and we lived with my grandparents. My grand-father was killed when I was seven or eight. But I had a nice upbringing, despite my mother's health and emotional problems:

she suffered from TB and never had any closure after her husband went down with the ship. My father's friends were nice, as were my aunts and uncles. A number of my uncles were role models, some better than others.

*   *   *

My father was definitely too strict. We lived in practically a paramilitary environment. I loved him and was close to him. He worked hard, spent a lot of time with me, was reliable and didn't avoid confrontation. But he had a temper. He was strict to the point of instilling fear in his family. I decided I didn't want my kids to be scared of me, but my older one was a bit.

*   *   *

He taught me the duty of a man is to love your wife and keep that relationship sacred.

*   *   *

He didn't spend a whole hell of a lot of time with me, but he was probably there more than I realized as a kid. I don't remember him missing a single baseball game. He did come to some of the scouting stuff even though he hated it. Spent all of his vacation time with us traipsing all around the country. I don't know if he enjoyed it. I know sometimes he didn't, but he still did it so he could spend as much time with us as he could. I didn't really know him well as a kid. I got to know him better as a teenager and as an adult. Now, I don't spend as much time as I probably should with him. He had a stroke a couple of years ago.

*   *   *

My father, in particular, was a black and white type of guy. There was right. There was wrong, and no bullshit. The shades of gray stuff? That didn't fly. I could see nuances, he did not. And he was willing to let you know that. He was very much a disciplinarian. He mellowed with time but was very willing to say, *Absolutely not. End of story. I don't care whether you like it or not. Go sulk, go cry, I don't give a shit.*

*   *   *

Both of them were very committed to our education and seeing us do better. Both sacrificed a lot. Actually when I was helping my parents put together their will a number of years ago, I was shocked at how much money they had amassed. My dad worked as a technician for RCA. Yeah, he had a share in a couple of restaurants here and there, but when I look at how much money they put away, I realized they saved it by not spending it. It's not like us. We'll walk home with big six figure bonuses every year. They were doing it on $30,000 a year. Like how do you have this much money put away? Go spend it on something.

*   *   *

For me, once a father, always a father. Good, bad or indifferent. Everybody's got one. I'm not sure you realize that until they're older. My kids are in their 30's. You're still their dad. You change, they change and presumably, if you live long enough, they'll find out as I did that there was small print on the diapers that I couldn't read that said, *Hey, if he lives long enough, you're going to be responsible for him.* That's what I went through with my dad. It's not easy. That's parents' retribution.

*   *   *

He marched me into the teacher the first day of school in first grade. He said, *Sister, if he gives you any trouble, box his ears.* I knew exactly where I stood. If I went home saying, *The teacher hit me for no reason* or *It wasn't my fault*, I wouldn't have had a chance.

40

*　　*　　*

He retired at age 62 after working hard all his life and being very committed to the company. But upon retiring he never stopped. He was involved with so many charities and church-related projects. Just never stopped. I never saw him sit down without paperwork in his hand, without a typewriter in front of him. If he watched any sports, he always had something else to do. Always. I never saw him stop once and relax. Not that he was a nervous Nelly fidgety guy that couldn't sit still. He just was always working. Some people just have that in their DNA. Always working.

*　　*　　*

I remember my father could be a hard ass. He's now mellowed with age, but he was tough on us and we were scared of him. My aunt and her second husband and their two boys, who were four and five, visited us for the first time. My aunt and uncle said, *We don't believe in disciplining the kids. We don't tell them No. What they're doing is really self expression.* They'd tear around the house and get into everything and just act like hurricanes. Us kids? We weren't supposed to play in the living room. My father would tell us to leave, and we got up and we got our asses out. There was no bullshit.

So in come these kids, our new cousins. It was like we had people visiting from the moon. My dad absolutely refused to give these kids any kind of slack. When they finally left, and I think they left a day early, my father said, *Don't come back.* There should have been a better way for him to handle that, but it was his house. He'd get in the kids' faces. *This is the way you behave here.* He didn't give a rat's ass what their parents thought, his sister-in-law and her husband. You don't act like that.

*　　*　　*

41

I was one of six kids and dad was a plumber. I never thought when I was growing up that it was a tough environment. I still feel like I never suffered, never was in need. But if you ask my brothers and sisters, they did without all kinds of stuff. I just never perceived it like that.

*   *   *

My father died when I was 2. My mother never remarried. I never had a father figure in my life. We were dirt poor. My first bike was one I made myself from spare parts. I stole coal off the trains leaving the coal mines to heat our house. I attended the same college where my mother scrubbed floors, where I have since started a scholarship fund in my late wife's name. I ran a grocery store when I was a kid. I remember beating up some guy who was trying to steal from my boss, the owner, who had cancer. I always worked. I always took on bigger challenges. I developed a set of balls at a young age. I had no choice.

*   *   *

My Father

Questions:

1   *What was your father like? Good points and bad points?*

2   *What influences did he have on you? What are the most lasting impressions?*

3   *Are you emulating what he did well? How?*

4   *Are you avoiding what he did poorly? How?*

42

Other Influencers

My mom had spunk. She was 5 foot 2 and I don't think anybody would ever mess with her, including my dad who had been a prize fighter for a while.

Uncle Harold was the business person. No nonsense business person. Very direct, hardworking. My father did just enough to get by. Uncle Harold always did what was necessary.

My step-father was a doctor. He was our family physician and my mother married him when I was in 7th grade. It was tough. He wasn't my father. He was not a sports fan. They had a child so I have a sister that is 13 years younger. There was always a little tension in the house. But he was a good man. I got to appreciate him much more as I got older, but I was never close to him. I don't feel like I grew up with a strong male role model. I've been fortunate once I got into the work world to have some very good role models and mentors. My maternal grandfather had a lot of influence on me. He was active in the community. I remember as a kid he would always talk to waitresses and stuff like that. I talk to anyone I see. I had two uncles I was pretty close to. But my father? I don't want to say he wasn't a main figure in my life but he wasn't. I view ourselves as totally different but we're probably not as different as I think.

*   *   *

I grew up without a father basically. My father was gone from when I was about a year old. I ended up living with my mother and grandmother and my mother's brother. And my mother's brother was in the house probably until I was about 6, and it probably saved my life. He was a really good guy and he was always like a father to me until he moved away and got married and had kids of his own. But even when he first got married, he lived close by for a couple of years. And he used to take me to football games and play catch. He basically fulfilled the roll of a father, which was terrific.

*   *   *

My uncle is a hardworking guy's guy with a good sense of humor. A little sarcastic but just a good guy who keeps his nose down and is very ethical. Highly ethical and that's one thing that I picked up from him and it's one thing that I want to pass on to my son. Above anything else you need to like what you see when you look in a mirror. And my daughter too. I don't mean how your makeup looks or whether you have a tan...you need to like what stares back at you and you need to be comfortable with that. You have to live with yourself. How you conduct yourself as a human being is the most important thing there is. My uncle spent as much time with me as he could. I still spend time with him. I probably spend more time caring for him than his two kids do. He actually has a daughter who doesn't speak to him.

*   *   *

I had a step-father who went out with my mother for quite a while but he didn't marry her until after my grandmother died. I guess I was in college by that time. But he dated my mother for a long time. He got me involved in little league baseball and did some fun things. Helped me with a couple of school projects but he

44

was pretty non-judgmental because he wasn't in a position to be particularly judgmental and kick my butt, so I did not have a lot of butt kicking growing up. I didn't have a lot of role models. I had a few, but I didn't have a lot and I didn't have somebody who was real stern. I grew up with two women. How I made it I don't know. I made it.

*   *   *

My mom was tough, direct, not afraid to use the paddle. And when the paddle came out you were going to get a whack in the ass. And it was okay. We probably deserved it. She was good at that. We called her The Warden. And in a good way. I had a good childhood. High expectations. I went to St. John of the Cross and Bishop McDevitt. Regarding college, it was expected you would go, it didn't matter where, and you were paying for it. So I ended up at Temple. And this notion now of trying to figure out what schools you can get your kids into so you can tell your friends at the country club they go to Yale versus Temple or whatever the hell it is. I guess we became exposed to that because of our success in our business careers. But it sure didn't come from my upbringing.

*   *   *

My mom had spunk. She was 5 foot 2 and I don't think anybody would ever mess with her including my dad who had been a prize fighter for a while. She grew up with three older brothers. She taught me to love baseball. She told me every single day of my life I could do anything I wanted, which is both a blessing and a burden because I thought, *How can I ever live up to that and live up to her expectations?* She was very politically involved so I'm a political junkie now. She was very outspoken; had a temper. Now as I look back, though I didn't know it at the time, she was probably depressed at times. She taught me to be open-minded.

45

*   *   *

And so I went into the service right after high school and I'll never forget this guy, Chief Master Sergeant Rosteran. This guy had been in the service for 35 years. He kind of took me under his wing. He was the first one who encouraged me to go to college. We were talking and he said, *Listen. What are you doing here?* I was enlisted. He said, *What are you doing here?* I said, *What do you mean?* He said, *You're too smart to be here. If you want to make a career in the service, you need to go and get your college degree and come back in as an officer. You should be an officer.* This was an enlisted person. He's a senior guy. I mean he had reached the highest level that he could possibly reach. And pretty powerful, too. He was a chief master sergeant, but he was every bit as powerful as some of the generals on the base. I understand power as the ability to get things done and influence and change the direction of things. So he was a very well respected person in that sense. But he helped me to think about my life and think about myself in different terms.

*   *   *

After I got out of the service, I did go into college. I went to LaSalle for undergrad and I think the next strong figure was Joe Finley, who was one of my accounting instructors. He was the one who really set my feet on the path that I'm on right now. He demanded a certain level of excellence and performance from me in my class work and expected me to achieve. When I was about to graduate from LaSalle, he hired me to work for him at Penn Mutual. He was the general auditor and he hired me into internal audit. That was my first job out of undergrad. And then I just rolled right into the MBA program at LaSalle. And as I was finishing the MBA program, he was the one that told me, *Look, you're not done yet.* I asked, *What do you mean?* He said, *You got to pass the exam.* I was like, *What are you talking about?* He said, *You have to pass the CPA exam and you got to get public*

46

accounting experience. I had no idea what public accounting was. Not really, not as a profession. That's how I actually ended up at Arthur Andersen.

*   *   *

Tom Weistack told me to call Jack McKay. He was friends with Jack and said that Jack would strongly consider me for a position at Arthur Andersen. So I called and tried to reach Jack, but instead got a hold of a Mike Mallon. Mike said, *Well, I don't know who you're talking about. We're not hiring. We're all done for the year. We're not hiring.* So I hung up the phone. I said to myself, *It's Tuesday and Tom Weistack told me to call Jack McKay. I have not talked to Jack McKay. I talked to Mike Mallon.* So I called back on Wednesday and I got Jack McKay. He said, *Yeah, Tom told me all about you. Can you come in tomorrow?* So on Thursday, I showed up at 9:00 and Jack and I sat and talked in his office for three hours. It wasn't like an interview. We were just talking, about my background and all this kind of stuff. At the end of the three hours, he looks at me and says, *So, you want the job?* I said, *Well, yeah.* He said, *Okay, come with me.* So he takes me downstairs and introduces me to Mike Mallon. He says, *Mike, this is Richard. Richard this is Mike. Mike, I just hired Richard. Process the paperwork.* So, that's how I got hired at Andersen and the rest is history. Sometimes you get lucky. You get a Jack McKay in your life.

*   *   *

I met Frank 18 years ago and since then, he's been like a father figure to me. He's probably the most fatherly person that I know, and I have to credit him with really helping me to understand what it means to be a father. That's why I'm telling this story, because Frank has 8 children, 31 grandchildren and he has 3 great grandchildren. Being a staunch Catholic, he and his wife were married for 57 years. He, Joe and Mike are the only people that I knew who had been with their wives for a long amount of

47

time and had done the kinds of things that we're talking about here. It really helped me to understand the importance of the fatherhood role and to think about the kinds of things I was doing and not doing in terms of fulfilling that role with my own son at the time.

*   *   *

Professor Joe. I used to call him *Laser Eyes*. He was tall and his hair was gray and silver. These piercing blue eyes. Whenever I would go to class, he would just kick my butt. You know, I can't put it any other way. He set the absolute highest standards. If I got an 85 that wasn't good enough. Because he said, *You can do better. How did you get this wrong? I know you know this stuff better than that. You answered this question correctly in class.*

*   *   *

I would spend summers at my father's house and he would take me to work with him and my uncle, whom I'm really close with now. Uncle Harold was the business person. No nonsense business person. Very direct, hardworking. My father did just enough to get by. Uncle Harold always did what was necessary. You would never see Uncle Harold not working. So you talk about work ethic, I think that was instilled in me through Uncle Harold and not necessarily through my father. My father would work hard and do whatever he had to do, but it wasn't like he was trying to build anything. Whereas Uncle Harold, on weekends and holidays, would pull up in the truck. Where everybody else was barbequing and partying, he would just be getting off from work and washing the paint off of his hands.

*   *   *

Well, you know I always just wanted my life to mean

something somehow. I think part of that might have to do with my oldest brother dying when I was fairly young. It just seemed like such a waste. He was about 21 years old at the time and I was probably 10 or 11 years old. But the thought that somebody could die at that young age really created a sense of urgency in me to do whatever it is I was going to do with my life. And to try to do something important and meaningful with it. He had a brain aneurism. So, if I reflect on it, that was one of the things that set a fire under me about being serious about whatever it is you're doing with your life notwithstanding your circumstances. I was determined to try to take it as far as I could take it, wherever that might be for me. Coming from where I came from, I was a huge success. Twenty-four years ago when I got a job in a Center City firm, that was something totally unimaginable to me.

*　　　*　　　*

My mom. We call her *Saint Jan* because we truly think she is a saint. She's very religious. She taught CCD, taught bible study and was a Eucharistic minister. She's now in a nursing home and has been for the last four years because of a couple of strokes that she's had. But probably the most loving and caring person you could ever know. I met a woman who told me, *Your mother is one of the most kind, loving, beautiful people I've ever come across in my entire life.* That's who she is. She just exudes love. Everyone who has ever known her just feels the passion and feels the love she gives out to everybody. And she is that person who loves to hug and embrace and stroke you and find out how your day went. And she was always there for us. She stayed home with all eight of us. I can't say enough about her. She's just an incredible person.

*　　　*　　　*

She went in the nursing home which she didn't want to do, but just she realized it had to be done because my dad just couldn't take care of her. She was on so much medication and she was

49

falling a lot. But within a year and a half, she was the president of the nursing home association. She was leading bible teachings; goes to Mass every day there; is best friends with the priest that comes in there; walks around and takes care of the people who are unfortunately getting ready to pass. My wife, when we first started dating and met my mother, said that one of the reasons she fell in love with me is because she saw a lot of my mother's quality in me. That's where I learned a lot of my caring, a lot of my compassion and treating everybody equal, regardless of race, religion, economic status. That's just who my mom was. She just saw people for who they were. And even if they were bad people, she saw the good in them, which is pretty powerful.

*   *   *

My parents were divorced when I was 10 years old. I grew up in Allentown, in a small but significant Jewish community. It was very rare for people back in the 50s in Jewish communities to get divorced, and it clearly was a major event in my mind and in my life. The scars that it creates never go away. It's always been a very strong motivation of mine to make sure that my marriage stays together and that it works as best as it can. I try to be with my kids as much as I can. So as a result, I've tried to live a balanced life. For example, when I went into government/politics in 1979 and became Deputy Mayor in 1980, one of my directives for myself was not to let anything happen or do anything that was going to ruin my marriage or my family. Probably three years into it, I realized that was starting to happen, and so I left. I could have stayed but my motivation was to make sure my family remained intact.

*   *   *

I grew up as a poor kid. My mom had 7 kids on welfare, yet I think I was spoiled. But we had nothing. So how can I think I was spoiled when really we had nothing? I think that kids have a ton

50

today and are spoiled. You know, this just wanting, wanting, wanting, where I would get hardly anything…I mean, really nothing. It just felt like I had a lot and I was the spoiled one in the family. What I think it came down to wasn't about the next thing my parents could buy for me. It was probably feeling like I got more time and attention than my other family members got.

*   *   *

Other Influencers

Questions:

1   Besides your father, who else has shaped your view of what a good parent should do?

2   Besides yourself, who else are your children learning from? What effects are they having on your kids?

3   Who are you learning from? Are there people you should be talking with about being a good father?

4   Are there other people with whom your kids should be getting more exposure? Less exposure?

Roles for Fathers

I guess at the end of the day, our number one job is to raise them such that they don't need us. That's what we're here for.

Someone said that the two things that are important as a parent is to anchor your children and to teach them to fly.

They didn't ask for you to create them. But once you do, it's your responsibility.

As a man, you've got a lot of responsibilities to your family. Number one is security. You have to make sure they're safe and provided for.

The role of a father is to provide guidance; to set an example; to be there; to love them; show them what's right and wrong.

*　　*　　*

A father is similar to a teacher. Fatherhood and teaching are both very selfish endeavors. To be good you need to accept the fact that you get as much back as you give. Being a good parent is very self-satisfying. It's ego gratifying. The ability to mold a life.

*   *   *

If you think because you brought a child into this earth and you're the male and you need to instill male values, I think you're missing the boat. I think a lot of people miss the boat. Actually they believe that as a male you must represent the prototypical male attributes and it's the woman that's going to do the other. I think that if you do that, you're really shortchanging your child. I think that there is a softness, a wonderful, emotional honing of every human being, male or female, and if you open up and give your child the opportunity to choose how they want to be, I think that's the best gift you can give. I think that fathering is an opportunity to expose to someone that you love all of the options. So pick and choose those traits, those attributes, those components that will make you what they need you to be based on their chemistry.

*   *   *

We were a mixed family and you always have a different situation in a mixed family. People have different opinions about the role a step-parent should play. Mine happens to be that the step-parent has a wonderful opportunity to become a coach, confidant, and a real asset to the kids. We have just a little more distance than the blood parent. Possibly we can be a little bit more objective and love them just as much and be just as much there for them - - possibly be there for them in a slightly different way. Probably not the major disciplinarian; it depends on the age of the kids.

When we got married, my kids were teenagers and far enough along so that somebody else coming into the house kicking butt and taking names might not have gone over so well. So I try to

53

be a steadying force, solid, dependable, willing to listen, not always to agree, and not always to say whatever they want to hear. Not necessarily just coming down and saying *No* all the time, but trying to explain the pros and cons. *Here's what you might want to look for and here's why your mother is telling you that and why it makes some sense.* With my kids, interestingly enough, I play pretty much the same role.

*　　*　　*

On the spectrum of very strict to what I will call liberal, I'm certainly a lot closer to the liberal side on raising kids. Maybe the conservative side on politics, but the liberal side on raising kids. I give them a fair amount of rope. If they abuse that, I will certainly pull that rope in, but I think that growing up is very much a learning experience. I think you have to learn by doing and you have to make mistakes. I try not to allow really big life-changing, life-threatening mistakes. I'll step in, but short of that, I try to encourage them to make a lot of decisions on their own. Get a lot of exposure. But I was always there to counsel, and I decided also that I wanted to be heard. Which means that you can't say too much and you can't say it for too long.

I always wanted kids who would at least listen and then use that information to make their own decisions. I figured out that I might not have the best-behaved kids, but I wanted real well-adjusted adults who are capable of standing on their own two feet and making their own decisions. When they went away to college they were used to making a lot of their decisions and hopefully weren't going to go totally off the deep end. I don't know whether I've been successful.

*　　*　　*

I would spend time telling them, not every little thing, but why they were being asked to do something or why it was

54

beneficial for them to do it. And some of that requires me not to be particularly judgmental. Also, I am able to have one child talk to me about what the other child or other children are doing. I'm able to do that because I don't always go in like a bull and take immediate corrective action. I want the information, so I got to find a way to get involved in such a way that I don't rat out the other one. If it's ever something really dangerous, then I can step in and do something. But most of the things are the typical things that you would expect of kids at the ages mine are. I just want to be aware of it so that I can have conversations about it but not necessarily conversations like, *Well you know your sister told me you were drunk 7 nights a week,* or whatever it is.

*　　*　　*

I didn't punish the kids very often. I just felt that some of the punishments typically meted out did not achieve the desire result. They don't change behavior. They may drive it underground but a lot of time it doesn't change the behavior a bit. It depends what the problem is. If it's really serious that's something else again, but I think what changes behavior, if anything, is the kid coming to the realization that, *Maybe this isn't good for me* or *Maybe it's not cool* or *I don't want to do it anymore for some reason.* And it's not, *I don't want to do it anymore because dad's going to beat me if he finds out* or *Gee, if dad finds me drinking and I'm driving the car, I guess he's going to take the car away.* There's certainly some merit there but does that stop the kid from drinking? Probably not. The kid goes off somewhere where dad doesn't see him, but it may stop him from drinking and driving the car.

*　　*　　*

In raising our kids, I'm not sure we had roles. There was no good cop - - bad cop type thing. If my kids had to describe it they would say that if they wanted understanding and a break, they

55

would probably talk to my wife. If they wanted the straight skinny, they would probably talk to me.

* * *

We had occasion, before our kids had their kids, to ask them if they would change anything in the way they were raised. And whether or not they thought the fact that we never took a vacation without them was strange. They said they did not think that was strange. They absolutely positively enjoyed it. The youngest one came back to me a while later. She called me up one day and said, *I want to thank you.*

* * *

My role versus my wife's role? Well, she's home so she has the primary role when it comes to basic care of the kids. She's there to get them off to school. She's there to welcome them home from the bus. She helps them with their homework. At least until I get home. She does all the stuff that any parent has to do when your kids are around during the day. During the summer, she's fulltime caregiver. My role is, well, chief provider, chief disciplinarian and enforcer of mom's dictates that get ignored because it's mom who says it. You know that whole thing about familiarity breeds contempt. My kids don't always treat my wife with the respect that they should. For a couple of reasons: that's just the way kids are and because she's not as forceful as maybe she should be sometimes in trying to get them to adhere to our rules. So that often falls to me to be the bad guy, which is a role that I accept although I try not to be unreasonable about it.

* * *

My kids would describe me as the enforcer. They would describe my wife, I hope, as a saint. They certainly would describe her as always there. Always supportive. Although her illness makes it hard for her to do everything she likes to do. And they recognize that. My son in particular. He's keenly sensitive to my wife's condition. And I don't even have to…all I have to do is say to him, *You know that mommy's sick,* and he'll start to tear up and he'll do whatever it takes to help her out.

*   *   *

As a man, you've got a lot of responsibilities to your family. Number one is security. You have to make sure they're safe and provided for. That's not necessarily something you have to shoulder alone. Your wife can help you with that but primarily as a man, that's your number one duty. And number two, you have to be loving to your wife. I think the way my father really showed his love for us was by showing his love for my mom.

*   *   *

I suppose if I rank my priorities, I'd rank my role as a father probably number two. My role as a husband probably is number one. But being a good husband is part of being a good father. If you don't respect your wife and love your wife and show your kids that you respect and love your wife, how are they going to respect you as a dad? So the two go together. But how do you show you love your wife without being sappy and dipshit? I'll do the hand holding, kissy huggy stuff in front of my kids. I show them. I tell them. I back her up, even if sometimes I think maybe she didn't do the right thing in telling them something or disciplining them. At least in front of them I back her up. And I try to treat her with the utmost respect around the house. Defer to her and do whatever I can to help her out especially with her medical condition. So I'll do as much of the cooking, the cleaning, the shopping, and I tell them the same, that we need to help mommy. And they've embraced that as something we all need to do as a family.

*　　*　　*

One of my challenges is judging how much influence I should use to help them versus letting them help themselves. I don't want to do more than I should, but also don't want to have them sit on unemployment and tell them, *Yeah, well you know, I did my job.* There is this phrase, *With great wealth comes great responsibility.* I believe, with great opportunity comes confusion. I mean, with the connections we have, we have huge opportunities to help our kids in whatever career path they choose. When do you stop doing that and let them earn it on their own? I don't know the answer to that yet. I'm trying to calibrate that right now.

How much can you continue to help them after you're "done"? Obviously if they're in jail, you bail them out. But you also don't have to buy them their first house necessarily. But the more you have and can give, the trickier it is to do.

*　　*　　*

I have worked at things I was not passionate about. I've made a good living doing things that I was not passionate about. My goal is to give my kids enough money that they don't have to be in that position. That they can pursue whatever they want.

*　　*　　*

The thing I think is important as a father is to provide a foundation of security. I thought it was important that our children have consistency in terms of where they lived, in terms of the daycare that they had, that they had the same babysitter/nanny for a long time. I wanted them to, at all levels, feel very secure. Someone said that the two things that are important, as a parent, is to anchor your children and to teach them to fly. So I want to make sure they are first anchored and feel very comfortable. And then the second thing is to teach them to be independent. So to teach them to fly. I think my kids are now just getting to the point where that's where our focus is. We're transitioning from, *Go take out the garbage,* to, *Here's your key to the house. Let yourself in when you come home.*

*   *   *

Certainly embedding core values is a critical role.

*   *   *

I want to make my kids tough. I want to make them tough physically and I want to make them tough mentally. Meaning they can get through a hard challenge. I don't want my sons picking fights to try to prove that they're tough or feel that they need to play sports because that will make them tough. But if they fall down I want them to be able to pick themselves up. We do expect them to work hard. Letting them fail is a hard thing. Knowing how hard to push is a hard thing.

*   *   *

I wonder if I'm overprotective. I've told this story and people shake their heads. When Zachary was born, I drove home with my hazard lights on from the hospital to our house.

*   *   *

Some parents provide private soccer coaches and personal trainers for their kids. It's embarrassing. First of all, it embarrasses me that I am in a group where I even know that that's going on. But on the other hand, it provides a very interesting discussion because my first reaction is it's something I'm repulsed by. On the other hand, if you peel it back, your kids have their own music teacher, or reading tutor. If your child happens to love that activity, and in order to continue to do that activity in the future they need

59

that type of tutoring, mentoring, or coaching, then you tend to provide it. But I struggle with that. As a father, my responsibility, obligation, and my desire is to provide for my children. Some of this other stuff is outsourcing fatherhood.

*   *   *

I do feel strongly that with fatherhood, you want to be their father, the best father, not a child's best friend. I've seen some instances where fathers try to be their kids best friends and I don't think that works at all. I mean, I would be hurt if my kids didn't like me, but I think they're going to be periods when they really, really don't. That's part of the job.

*   *   *

In my generation, we want to be more involved with our kids, and we do spend more time with them. Games. Activities. We want to do more things with them and I think that's okay. But there's a big difference in being involved and trying to be their best friend versus being their parent.

*   *   *

I want to be more present, more of a guide in their lives than I felt that my dad was. I want to provide security for them. Security in every way. I want them to be safe. I think that's my job. I want them to feel personally secure so that they can take chances, have fun, be creative, learn in the way they like to learn.

*   *   *

My role as a husband is really closely related to my role as a father. The more they can see how much I love their mother, the more they feel loved. And I think when she and I fight, I think it's okay as long as we continue to love each other and that shows up.

Really important that the kids see no matter what, my wife and I love each other.

*   *   *

My perspective on being a father is that it involves a lot of coaching. Helping them find themselves, and learn love and acceptance. I also think I'm a provider.

*   *   *

I talked to some guys who want to give their kids enough money so that they are not saddled with doing what they don't really want to do in order to support themselves. I don't feel compelled to do that. I think that violates the first principle around what my role is, which is providing self security and self esteem. Given my background, I worked my way through school. It's hard for me to imagine that they would develop self esteem if everything was just given to them. I don't feel like I have to provide in that way. I just have to make sure they have good food and shelter. We made a commitment to their private school but I think that's an add on. I've seen people completely set up their kids financially and they're great kids. But it's just not who I am.

*   *   *

One of my roles is to figure out how to help them learn the way they learn best. People learn in different ways. They have different personalities. Everybody loves to learn. We're born with a desire to grow. That's taken away from most of us as we grow up. The school system now focuses on grades, and so to me it's important to support them in the ways that they love to learn. My son is very physical, very active. He is quick as a whip in math but if you sit him down in school, and he has to do 20 math questions, he is so distracted by his friends that he has to come home to do it. He's always moving. He learns so much more when he does. My

61

daughter is very creative and very quiet. How she likes to learn is to go in her room, to read or draw or in some way be creative. I am not trying to force them to learn as I learned. Or as I was forced to. I want them to achieve a love of learning forever.

*   *   *

That 18 or 19 year old transition to 22 or 23 is as intense as the midlife transition. Yet we don't tend to recognize that. Instead we send our kids off by themselves. A lot of them commit suicide. Midlife transition is not easy, but their transitions in their teens and twenties are incredibly tough times as well.

*   *   *

They need to earn and deserve some responsibility before they leave home. It's like dating. I absolutely want them to be dating before they go to college. I don't want the first time they fall in love to be when they're away on their own.

*   *   *

Our job as parents is to prepare them for the world. Sometimes that means determining when they get privileges, and when they don't get privileges. But also making sure they get an opportunity to experience and grow so they can be self sufficient. I guess at the end of the day, our number one job is to raise them such that they don't need us. That's what we're here for. To make sure that they will have happy, healthy lives without mom and dad. To me, that really kicks in when they go to college. Because by the time they go to college, outside of providing financial support or just moral support occasionally, we're done. They're adults. They're on their own.

*   *   *

At that point, once they go to college, outside of giving them money, we're a safety net. Right and wrong, they will have learned a long time ago. Morals, they will have learned a long time ago. So our job is to get them ready, and that's my demarcation line. They have to be very strong, self-sufficient, mature, moral adults when they leave home. It's guiding, it's allowing mistakes before they're too costly. They are some of the things I've learned from watching my family grow up. Watching the mistakes I thought my parents made, as well as things they did well.

*   *   *

The kids are our first priority. Taking care of them is number one. When we had the first kid, it's kind of, game over. That's what we're going to do. I think that was something that was instilled in us as we were growing up. There are a lot of things you have to sacrifice. And I looked at them as a sacrifice. It wasn't like, *Oh I have the kid and I don't care about that stuff I had to give up.* No, I miss that stuff. But now, you go in with your eyes open. They didn't ask for you to create them. But once you do, it's your responsibility.

*   *   *

I think there are a lot of different ways to raise your children. You can always argue what's better, what's worse till the cows come home. I think at the end of the day, you have to love your kids and you have to love them more than you love anything else.

And if you love them that much, you're going to do good things for them. Your good things may be different from my good things, but if you love them and you want the best for them, everything else should work. It may work at different degrees but it will work. If you don't care about your kids, it doesn't matter what you do. It won't work. If you don't love them, it won't work. And

63

in terms of raising them to be good people, if you don't care about them or if you just throw money at them, it doesn't work - - look at Hollywood.

*   *   *

And then once my son was born, it really helped to set the tone for my life, for the kind of parent that I wanted to be. With my son, I wanted to make a better life for him, do the kinds of things I needed to do to make sure that he had a shot at a better life than I had when I was a kid.

*   *   *

My son used to say to me, *I never want to do what you do. You work too hard.* You know, the things that kids say when they're teenagers. Now that he's out on his own, it's amazing. His wife tells me that he is just like me. In fact, he asked me to be the best man at his wedding. That was an honor.

*   *   *

My wife and I talked about this early on. I can say that I made a conscious decision to drive a stake in the ground and say I can't do anything about what happened in the past. I can't do anything about what my parents are or who my grandparents were. I can't think about my ancestry and all these kinds of things. I don't know anything about that. I can't do anything about it. But I can do something about what happens from this point forward. So that 400 years from now, if there's a picture of me hanging on the wall, if they can't go back any further than me, I want those people, whoever they are 400 years from now, to be able to say, *That was my great, great, great, great, great whatever, grandfather and his name was Edmund Green, and this is what he did. He started it all. This is how we got to where we are.* I do remember having that conversation with my wife even before we got married. I said, *Look this is the deal that I'm trying to put together here.*

*   *   *

You're going to be different. You need to hear that from somebody, somebody telling you what they see that you can't see in yourself. That's what fathering is all about. That's what mentoring is all about as well. I think Frank Palamara told me that at one time. He said, *You don't understand. You can't see what I see. You're not old enough.*

*   *   *

I'm not speaking for the whole race of people. But from a cultural standpoint, I think that there are a lot of African American males who are growing up in these single parent families, with the mother, no father. A mother caters to them, so they grow up thinking that the role of the woman is just to take care of me. And they just continue that into adulthood as an expectation.

But part of the role of the father is to, first of all, provide a role model. It's one thing for me to sit here and say to you, *You need to get your ass up out of that bed and go to work every day.* But it's something all together different for you to see a person do that day in and day out, year in and year out, for the entire course of your life. Up at 4:30, 5:00 in the morning. Coming home at 11:30, 12:00 at night, day in and day out, just hammering away at it. I'm sure you saw that with your father. You see that and you look at that. He doesn't have to say anything. You just know. That's the template. If you want to have your own life and be your own man and make your way in the world, that's what you do.

And it's not something you can talk somebody into doing. They have to see it. They need a template. They need a role model. They need somebody they can see and say, *Oh yeah, I know, I personally know a guy who did that. I personally knew a guy who sat in that kind of chair. I personally know a guy who was CFO and you can see the fruits of his labors, and you go to his home, and you can see what he's done.* It's not just talk. You know what I mean? So it's the difference between reading in a book versus experiencing it firsthand. So for my son, one of the things that he told me was that a lot of his friends can't understand him being the way he is. A lot of them grew up in those kinds of environments, single parent mom, taking care of them, doing everything for them. These guys are 25, 26, 27, 28 years old still living at home with their mom. Meanwhile, he's been out on his own for the last 3, 4, or 5 years. And so he says that one of the things that helped him was seeing me do that, and he wanted to do it for himself.

*   *   *

What is my role as a father? I came up with a few words that might seem contradictory. The first one I put out there is a friend. I think to my son, I'm his best friend. And you sit there and say, *How can you be a best friend and a father at the same time?*

Some say you can't be a friend to your child, and I think I challenge that every single day with him because I really do believe I'm his best friend. I love being with him, love doing things with him, love exploring things with him. Just love hanging out with him and whenever we find ourselves in that moment, just having a great time and learning from each other. But also, knowing when I need to play that other role, which is more of a defined father, where I need to make sure I guide him in the right way, and give him some basic principles that will help him later in life. Being a disciplinarian sometimes and making sure that I'm setting a good example as a provider for our family, too. And most people would think that that's a tough role for me. But actually I think it's a tough role for him to balance between those two aspects, but he does it really well.

66

*　　*　　*

Look at the characteristics of what a friend is. It's somebody that you can rely on, that you trust, that you have a mutual respect for. And a father? There are a lot of commonalities, so maybe we aren't so different from a friend. Maybe it just comes down to how you deliver a message. A father being an authoritative figure and a friend being more collaborative in an equal relationship. But both, I think, are based on the common principles of trust and respect.

My father, he passed away when I was 13. I don't know how to be a dad, but I know how to be a decent friend, so maybe I'm applying those principles of doing what I'm good at? I'm good at that dual role as friend and dad. I can use those common principles of trust and respect as a framework and a platform. I'm not so sure I can go all that wrong.

*　　*　　*

Going out and throw a ball around. Going to a ballgame. It's fun. You have these moments that something else brings, comes into your life. You could just be watching TV. It gives you that "aha" moment too. We were watching some stupid show called *The Nanny* just because it's summer time and not much else is on. They went through this game of trying to guess what your kid likes best interacting with you. And one kid said wresting; one said something else. I asked my son, *What is it for you that's the best thing?* He goes, *Everything dad. I can't really think of one thing; just everything.*

*　　*　　*

I'm not holding back. I'm not guarding myself as some fathers might. I believe in letting their kids see a human, fun loving, goofy side of yourself. Not trying to maintain a façade just because you're the parent and he's the kid. I never saw that other side of my dad. My son is going to see all the blemishes but also the upside and all that good stuff, too. I'm not afraid to expose him to those things because I think he's great at self regulating. He doesn't go wild; I mean, this kid, he gets it. He's shaped a pretty neat style and personality and characteristics of his own. Now, what I fear, is that I don't want him to be me either. I just don't want him to say, *I'm doing things to please you and replicate you.* I haven't seen that. I think he is developing his own style. He'll even correct me. Like, *Dad, that's not right.* I'll bust on somebody and he'll have none of it. He'll just stop and won't participate in it.

*   *   *

I think the other thing is taking a lot of accountability and responsibility for setting the tone in my household. I know when things aren't going well at work, I can bring those things home. If I had a tough day, I can bring those things home. When I do, I can tell you that the household is different and my wife is different. My son is different. I'm aware of that. I'm aware I'm the one setting the tone for the household, at least I think I am. So when I'm there, it's important to be there. I'm there but with an attitude about trying to be fun, of trying to find a moment just to be there and just to talk to him when wants to talk. And going out on the front lawn and throwing the ball around for 10 minutes. My wife's quieter than I am. At least the tone I want the household to have, I have taken responsibility for that. I think most every situation, most every house, has its tone. I have a big impact on it and I'm going to throw that on my shoulders. And it's fun.

*   *   *

My dad was a great influence on me. I think I'd do a few things differently. I try, for example, to be more expressive because it's a different era. I try to be more expressive about telling my children that I love them or kissing them goodnight. Not

68

that he didn't kiss me goodnight, but just in terms of being a little bit more demonstrative about that. My son has picked that up too. I mean he is willing to be affectionate and give a hug and all that kind of stuff, which is good.

*   *   *

The ability to have the emotional strength to deal with conflict when it needs to be dealt with is learned through both marriage and through childrearing. My first daughter went through a very difficult time from age 12 to 18. It was hard just trying to figure out how to manage some of those conflicts. It's incredibly humbling. There are a lot of mistakes that you make along the way and you hope in the aggregate you can make more right decisions than wrong ones. But sometimes you wonder which outweighs the other.

*   *   *

One motto that I try to hold, that I learned from my own coaches, is the mantra of *Praise in public and criticize in private.* I practice this in my business life all the time. If I feel that I've got something that's a negative assessment of my kid or a negative assessment of somebody who works for me, I feel I owe it to them not only to tell them in person but to sit them down privately so they're not embarrassed by my giving them that negative assessment at the dinner table. Not in front of their friends or the other kids. If he does the same thing seven times, then I will. But my first approach, if I have bad news or the bad mail to deliver, it would be private. *Let's go take a walk; let's go out in the backyard; let's sit in your room for a second; I got to talk to you about something.* That's part of the coach in me.

*   *   *

I had been coaching varsity soccer for about four years, and

69

I remember calling up my high school coach, who by that time had coached for 40 years. And I said, *Mr. Moulton, I'm really struggling here. One year I feel like I'm close to the team, and sometimes I feel like I'm making the mistake of being too close. Then I back away the next year and I tend to be more distant and then I don't feel like I'm getting as much out of my players as I should. I can't figure out this balance between closeness and distance.* I remember him saying to me, *When you figure that out, that balance, it's time for you to quit.* He said when you think that you've got that one solved, that's your first sign to get out of the game; because you never get that one solved.

I think this applies in raising my own children, too. What does it mean to have a friendly relationship with your kids, with a sense of humor? At the same time you're still in a position of authority or guidance and coaching. You're still in a different role and trying to strike that balance between playfulness and fun, and at the same time maintaining a role that is different from that. That balance is hard to strike and it's never perfect. I think the message that Don Moulton gave me about coaching the soccer team resonated all the way through my coaching career and it still resonates on the parental side as well because you're always trying to strike a balance between warmth, love, caring; and at the same time, you're a parent, you're not a peer.

In other words, what he was saying is that part of your job as coach is to continue to work at it and try to figure out what that balance is. Don't think you've got it. Don't give up, one. And two, don't think you've got it. You always have to work on it because it's always going to change.

*   *   *

We got in from a party and I just flicked on the TV and the replay of the U.S. Open was on. That run that Tiger made was on. The two young kids went to bed and my wife went to bed, and my two other daughters were just sitting with me. And I love Tiger. I just think he elevates everybody's game. So they said, *Who are we rooting for here, dad*? I said, *Tiger,* and every time he makes a putt, they'd clap, they'd high five, they would be running around doing cartwheels and getting all crazy. And any time any of the other players hit, they would boo, so they got all into it. So the next day I brought in clubs I got a while back. So we're all outside Sunday morning hitting little air golf balls all over the front lawn. They were excited to watch the final U.S. Open which was really neat. So it's the first time I ever saw them really get involved and interested in sports.

*   *   *

Key is spending time with your kids and being there for them. My wife and I often talk and the biggest fear we have is that our children grow up and are not open enough to talk to us about anything. Whether it be sex, whether it be drugs, whether it would be school, whether it would be this person or that person. When my daughter comes home and there's a kid who was picking on her, we would pick up the phone and we'd call that mom with my daughter right there and talk to that mom. It showed her that when she tells us something, we're going to react. We're going to take care of her. We had her in the room there for the reason that we wanted to make sure that she'd come to us with anything. This was back in kindergarten. Well, nothing was done. The kid kept picking on her, so again, we sat my daughter down and we called the principal and said, *Listen. It's just not acceptable.* My daughter saw that. That's the kind of openness that we want to have. So directionally, what we really want to be able to have is the kids feeling comfortable enough to bring anything and everything to us.

*   *   *

I don't think I was a great father. I wasn't a role model father. I think I was a careful father. I'm probably right in the normal range. How boring is that? As I reflect back on it, I'm not sure, despite the efforts that my wife and I made, we did much more than supply the shelter, the food, the clothing, the safe environment, and then just loved the kids. That's your role. As I look back, if I thought I was influencing my kids to have this value or that career ambition or this desire, then I would be wrong. They grew up to be their own people and I wouldn't want it any other way. So I think sometimes, at the end of the day, all I really did was provide the shelter, the food, the clothing, the love, and a safe environment, and then loved them. Beyond that, it was all for my benefit. Not theirs. You know, I played with the kids when they were little and we had a tremendous amount of fun. I participated with them in their activities as they got a little older. School, their sports, sometimes their friends, travel and all that kind of thing. I think it was as much for my benefit as theirs. I mean, I really had a good time with it and loved doing it.

*   *   *

I guess the most important thing you do as a father is protect and provide for your family. And you make some sacrifices that affect the family. Some of the sacrifices were in order to provide for them. You didn't see them as much as you would like to and that's an equation that's always challenging to balance. After that, you want to nurture them. I think you do have an opportunity to influence them in things that are important. And one thing I've stressed to them is to always work hard.

*   *   *

I see my role as a person who carries us through a storm. My own life growing up was very difficult, and so I try to be a sanctuary when times are tough. And also being a cheerleader. I love telling my daughter I love her, and then she tells me back that she loves me too. I read and hear of people being afraid to say, *I love you.* So every day we reinforce the love we feel.

72

I let my kids know how difficult certain areas were for me. I don't come off as a know-it-all. I had a problem with chemistry. I'm not mathematical minded. I think in terms of relationships with employees and clients, that was a strength. I try to help them see where they're strong and teach them there's no one who's perfect. Everybody has some flat sides.

*　　*　　*

Be sensitive to what your child feels is embarrassing. I was making these corny jokes in front of her friends. She got me off on the side and said, *Dad please stop that. You're embarrassing me.* I said, *That's my job. That's what dads do.* Probably not the right approach.

*　　*　　*

My son was about 21, 22 and he was having a hard time just getting focused on things. I, being the coaching dad, gave him my advice. And he said, *Well, dad. The only thing you have to remember is, they're just your answers.* What does that mean? You can put it out there for your children to pick it up. They can do something with it or not. If they don't want to do that, at least you've talked it through. You have to give them the opportunity to fail on certain things. A friend of mine is having a very difficult time. He does all the wrong things. He's a very successful cardiac surgeon. He's got the worst relationship with his son. It's a tragedy. He'll call me up. *What do you think?* I said, *You got to let it go. He doesn't want to do it. You want him to go into medical school and he wants to be a chef. You're ruining your relationship.*

*　　*　　*

My son and I, for my 60th birthday, went down to Cabo.

We played golf and went ocean fishing. And we met the guy who managed the Beatles, and his wife. We were hanging out with these folks around the bar and dinners because they put you at the same table and you get to meet people. So toward the end of the week, this woman said, *You know I've been looking at you two all week and you have such a fantastic relationship. You seem to enjoy each other.* And Bryan said, *Well, I kind of matured some and my dad loosened up. Kind of met part way.*

*   *   *

Provide the framework they need in life skills and a safe place to make mistakes. If you make mistakes in sixth grade, your mistakes are smaller. The older you get, the bigger the mistakes are. So at this stage in the game I'm trying to provide a framework for them to safely make mistakes and learn. My mother-in-law and her other daughter have a co-dependent relationship. She never let go. Her daughter's in her 30s and she still is incapable of navigating the world without her mother there. That's one of those self-fulfilling things. Mother actually catches her and says, *See, you can't do without me. You're not smart enough. You're not good enough. It's good I was here to help you out.* That's not what you want to do as a parent. I view it as okay for them to make mistakes that they're going to make so they're ready to meet the world.

*   *   *

Help them to like themselves. To me, if you have an appropriate level of confidence and you like who you are, the world's a good place. If you don't, if you don't have a level of confidence, if you don't like yourself, then bad things happen.

*   *   *

I think people need to reinvest in their own family

74

relationships and marriage relationships. I think why marriages fail is that there is so much to do and one person may end up being the caregiver, one person might end up being not as much involved. I see it more now, more crisply in my grandchildren than I did in myself. It wasn't as obvious then as it is now.

*   *   *

We've always had very strong family customs and one of the things that the kids talk about is our vacations. I wanted to do everything with them. I couldn't stuff enough things into the week or two weeks of vacation whether it was at the shore, or we went away, or we went and visited family. I think my kids got exhausted from going on vacations. I probably over-planned them. It probably balanced more when they got to be pre-teens and early teens, because then sports and other outlets provided enough dad time on any given day or week or month.

*   *   *

We get into some pretty competitive family things. We're a very competitive family. You don't want to play charades with us unless you're really well versed and ready to fight. We once played a game of Spoons. My brother-in-law lunged at me and broke my kitchen table. We had to get a reinforced table the next time he came down. We play all sorts of card games and we really enjoy doing things with our kids.

We were always close from the time they were born and they always knew they could always come home. One of our family rules is it doesn't matter where you are or what the circumstances: if you are in need of help, you just have to call. There's unconditional support and backup and love. If you need something you can always call and, unfortunately, all three of my kids made use of that rule at different times. But they knew that there was an unquestioned backup and support in our family. I

75

think that's something that you should as a father pass along. You provide support not in the traditional sense but the kind of support where the kids feel totally at ease and they have a place where they can deal with whatever issue they need to deal with without fear of any kind of retribution.

*   *   *

With all my kids, I always tried to find time to do things individually not just with all three, whether it was sports, scouts, charity or volunteerism. When we used to do things like "Christmas in April," both my two older children spent a day with me doing volunteer work. I thought it was important and I didn't have to drag them to do that. I think they quickly learned the importance of helping people.

*   *   *

My son had a weight problem when he was in his preteen years which really was pretty significant. He dealt with it himself mostly and with some help from my wife. He was very smart. He was taking five AP classes at a top level high school. Probably the weight issue made it hard for him to have friends, but he was such an intellect. As a sophomore in high school, he was probably pushing 250 pounds. Today he weighs 155. He lost all the weight on his own. Weight Watchers and training and this, that and the other. He changed high schools, lost the weight and maintained the academics. High school had to be the worst years to be dealing with that. I probably wasn't as much help as I could have been. Not sure how I could have been more helpful because weight was something I never had to deal with. I was the smallest guy in my eighth grade class.

*   *   *

If I step back and think about my kids when they were

little, clearly my first priority and focus was work, bringing money into the household and getting the career where it needed to be. I was with him as often as possible and certainly for every party and as many baseball games and soccer games and everything else I could make. But, you know, there were situations when I was traveling and somebody's birthday came along and whatever. That was just kind of the way it was. My wife and I have different memories of how much I was there. She tells interesting stories about being a single mother and that kind of stuff. The kids look at her cockeyed like, *Yeah you're exaggerating. Get a grip. He was here a lot more than you think he was.*

*   *   *

I coached soccer until I was made to quit by my wife. One year I was coaching and I had my two younger kids on the team. They were 9 and 10. There was this kid, Joey. And all the parents are lined up on the sidelines and I'm yelling, *Joey, kick the ball.* I was a pretty active coach. I would like run up and down the sidelines. *Joey, kick the ball. Joey, kick the ball.* **Joey, kick the goddamned ball!** And she said all the parents' eyes shot at her and she just kind of looked like, *I don't know him.* So I became the treasurer of the league after that. That was my last year of coaching. I was a little intense.

*   *   *

Spend as much time as you can with them. I know it's tough sometimes. You get home from work and you're beat up. It's 7:00 at night. You know you got to get them ready for bed and you got to get them showered. But just by getting them ready for bed and getting them showered is spending time with them. And I do that pretty much every night. I help out with one or two or all three depending on how my wife's day is going.

*   *   *

I think a big part of being a good dad means being good to yourself. You can't neglect yourself by being unhealthy or showing them it's okay to just sit around and smoke cigarettes and drink beer all damn day and not be out there and be active. You need to be healthy and good to yourself, mind and spirit and body, to be a good dad.

*   *   *

I am the provider of financial security. I work hard, partly so my wife doesn't have to work, and can be as committed to the kids day-to-day as she is. An important role is to show my kids how much I love my wife. I try to give my kids a model of stability and unity with my wife and strength as a family unit. Nothing would ever cause my marriage to break up, and this provides the love and support for my kids to grow and thrive. I am away a lot with work during the week. But I try not to work on weekends. Weekends are for my wife and kids. I give my wife a break by doing the shopping and driving the kids around.

*   *   *

My role is to teach my kids right from wrong, character, judgment and the importance of education.

*   *   *

I was the disciplinarian. I didn't hit them but I would raise my voice and intimidate them. They were always respectful to my wife and me. They knew we wouldn't tolerate rudeness or disrespect.

*   *   *

I tried to be a coach and point out options. I tried not to direct them and tell them what to do. I would remind them of lessons learned and told them when they were going down the wrong path, but I tried to avoid saying, *I told you so.*

*   *   *

I'm trying to help my kids do what I try to do. To recognize there is good and bad; to choose what to keep and what to let go. To be self-aware, to be analytical and to make good choices, instead of being rash or overly emotional or narrow-minded.

*   *   *

A father should be a teacher, a coach. I'm not talking about academics – that's what schools are for. I'm talking about life.

*   *   *

I try to transfer as much knowledge and wisdom as I can to my kids. How? I tell them stories about how I grew up: the rough background; the gangs, violence and drugs that were all around. Every day I spent an enormous amount of energy planning how to get back and forth to school without getting ripped off or beaten up. Every day. But this is part of their history. They need to hear it. They will face their own problems and they need to learn how to handle them.

*   *   *

Despite my tough upbringing, I was told I could do anything I wanted to do and become whatever I wanted to be. I am trying to help my kids develop this same vision.

*   *   *

Teaching is more telling. I want my kids to have empathy. I want them to put themselves in other people's shoes and relate to them. I want them to ask questions, and listen - - really listen - - in order to know what is true. But I try to do this by doing it myself. I listen to my kids. I ask them a lot of questions. I try to help them self-discover. I do this with them but I also let them see me do the same in how I treat adults.

*   *   *

My daughter hit me with a question about pre-marital sex. I didn't lecture her and I didn't attack her with a ton of questions. But I didn't let her (or me) off the hook either. I tried to help her think through the impact of certain decisions. The impact of AIDS, STDs, pregnancy and giving up plans for a career.

*   *   *

I am a mediator between my wife and kids. She's overbearing, but she is responsible for what the kids have become, which are young adults that I would give my life for. They have me wrapped around their fingers. I'm their pal. Outside of questions about fashion, I get the first call.

*   *   *

My role is to listen first, not necessarily to fix a problem or even give advice. They might have an issue with money or an issue with their mother. They don't hesitate to come to me.

*   *   *

One of my biggest roles has been to provide a fulfilling educational environment. My girls picked expensive colleges. One picked an expensive law school. But I never complained about spending on their education.

*   *   *

Disciplinarian. I was the bad guy. My wife always told them, *Ask your father*. I was also the problem solver. Even now, when the kids call with a problem, they ask for me. When they call to say, H*ello*, they ask for my wife.

*   *   *

Roles for Fathers

Questions:

1   *What are the most important roles a father should play?*

2   *What are the most prominent roles you are playing?*

3   *How well are you performing in these roles?*

4   *What can you be doing better?*

5   *Is there anything you should do differently? Are you going to change anything? How?*

Wives and Mothers

She was more disciplined with the kids and set certain requirements. I would give in.

My wife and I have many similar values. I think we want the same things for our kids and have the same objectives. The tactics can be very different.

My kids would go to my wife with their problems. She is a better listener. I tend to analyze and provide solutions, but often kids don't want solutions.

I think from our wounds come our gifts. I think I'm much better because of my first marriage, which was a struggle.

I don't think you can father independent of a mother when a mother is in the picture. I fathered and mothered collectively when I was widowed for a 4 ½ year period so I had the morbid, wonderful opportunity of being both father and mother. The problem with that simply is that there is no good guy, bad guy scenario. The last thing you want is your child to go to bed without a wonderful hug and kiss. Sometimes it's hard to be the disciplinarian and nurturer at the same time when there's only one. That's why parenting is, by definition, two people.

*   *   *

How would my kids describe my wife? We've got two sets of kids that we're talking about. My kids would describe my wife, who is not their mother, as immature and somewhat of a whack job and possibly irrational, which may go along with whack job. They would also say inconsistent. Her own kids would also describe her certainly as loving, concerned, quite hands-on and micromanaging, but very inconsistent and also a whack job.

How do they define whack job? Inconsistency has a lot to do with it. My wife grew up in a family of 6 kids. Her father was a Navy man and basically he didn't take any static at all. He wasn't one of these guys who said, *I love you.* I happen to like him. We have a fine relationship, but he was tough. It was his way or the highway, and I think he probably yelled a fair amount. Six kids. To be heard he had to yell probably. So my wife tends to yell and raise her voice and fly off the handle, and I don't always think she's rational. And then the next moment she'll have her arms around them. She's very up and down. There are very high highs and then low lows. I'm not talking about depression. The lows tend to be anger or impatience. She's very back and forth, whereas I'm very even keeled. Yet the teenagers are doing the same thing. Not the son so much but the daughter. She's got the teenage disease of a 15 year old girl, but mom's the same way. So that's why they think she's whacky. She will come down hard on them and say, *You're not going out next weekend.* Over just the littlest of things, *You're not going out next weekend. Both of you, you're in for the whole weekend.* When next weekend comes, they're out both nights because she doesn't follow through.

*   *   *

Have my wife and I always been on the same page in terms of what to do with the kids; how to raise the kids; what to impart to the kids? In general, yes. She was more disciplined with the kids and set certain requirements. I would give in. That's even true now. I always wanted to make it easier for my kids than my wife did. It was never anything that got in the way, but she says that, to this day, I'm too easy, I give in, I coddle -- and she's probably right. It's my personality. I'm that way in business. I'd rather give in on a point than to fight it to death. That's just me.

*   *   *

We don't have a good guy, bad guy or good cop, bad cop thing going. But we also didn't do any of this, *You wait till your father comes home* stuff. It was dealt with, whatever the issue was, positive or negative. But I would suggest that my kids and my wife would all tell you I'm the stronger personality on the team when raising the kids.

I think what's required has changed with time. When the focus was on raising the kids when they were little, it was closer to her core competency than it was mine. As they grew older, we changed roles a little bit. And by the way, I've never had this conversation with her, but she would probably say exactly the same thing. We've never talked about. It just happened naturally. So as your kids get older, what they need is different and it may mean that the other parent has to be stronger, because that's what he or she's better at. It's not father versus mother. It could be the other way around.

*   *   *

My wife and I, we're in a different position. We sometimes lock horns about how to raise the kids. I don't think it's good for the kids. But I think we agreed that we have the same goals for our kids. My wife and I have many similar values. I think we want the same things for our kids and have the same objectives. The tactics can be very different. And that I know is one of the problems that we're trying to understand and deal with ourselves and then deal with our kids as well.

*　　*　　*

I think we both had the same approach to discipline. She was as tough or tougher than I, but where we differ now is when it's time to give them some rope. Her first reaction is, *No*. And mine is, *Wait a minute, let's talk about it*. And then she comes around pretty quickly. Either because I overpower her in the conversation or whatever. But that's the only place we'd ever disagree.

*　　*　　*

I think she has been such an incredible influence on me as a father. Certainly in terms of raising our kids. I think of who influenced me most on my being a father, and my wife is the person I feel had the biggest influence.

She's always guided me and mentored me in ways that make me a better father. She has instilled a certain structure in the way we have raised our kids. I think that has worked out very well for us. I don't think I would have instilled the same structure. But our kids seem to be doing well in school and we get a lot of feedback from others about their behavior, and I think that has to do with the structure that she set up and helped me with. I would have been a lot less structured. She also helped me become more open-minded with my kids. One of the things I struggled with is I have a certain image of what it may take to be successful or what it means to be successful, but each one of our kids is very different. And they all require a different type of fatherhood approach, and she really helps me see that and helps me deal with them in a much

85

more open-minded way. She is extremely value-driven and value-oriented, not so much from a religious sense, but she'll make a lot of decisions that are value-based. She helps instill those in our kids and helps them make the right decisions.

The other way she really helps me is, she helps me evolve. She evolves quickly and she helps me evolve quickly, so as the kids' needs change and we need to change, she's the one that helps push that along. Those are all incredibly helpful attributes that I think her father had.

*   *   *

Do I feel like we're on the same page in terms of raising the kids? Is there tension? Are there different orientations? Is there sort of a tug of war sometimes between my wife and me in terms of how we influence the kids or decision making pertaining to the kids? For the most part, we're on the same page. I think there are different things we emphasize a little bit given our different backgrounds. I think there are a lot of things that my wife influenced me on. She's very hardworking. She also very demanding. She sets high expectations with them especially with regard to their work ethic. Where she came from she didn't play a lot of games. So if there is any tension, it's the tension between how much we push them and how much we coddle them. We go back and forth sometimes. I'll push one of them or the other a little bit harder, and she'll think I'm pushing a little too hard. And vice versa. It's probably where the greatest tension is.

*   *   *

Some of the children and their behaviors she can deal with and I can't, and there are definitely some behaviors that I can deal with that she can't. There are definitely things where I am tougher. I'm more abrupt at times and I'm a little bit more definitive. But I think they think their mom can be tough also. And I think she disciplines them on certain things more than I do.

*　　　*　　　*

I think kids are incredibly sensitive to things that are unspoken, like behavior, attitude and how people treat each other. Even if they can't articulate it because they're very young, they pick up on those things. I try to be incredibly careful. I try to teach my daughter as a woman she has every opportunity a man does. But if I don't treat her mother with that kind of respect, that message will get completely lost no matter how many times I say it. I tell my daughter I love her no matter what, that I have unconditional love. But if it doesn't show up in how I treat her mother, she might not trust me, especially if I say I do and it's obvious I don't. They can pick up when it's disingenuous. I think it's a role model for my son. I want my son to be a gentleman. I want my son to listen to his mom and show her the respect that we need to show each other. I could talk about that forever, but unless I'm doing that, he's not going to get it.

*　　　*　　　*

I think from our wounds come our gifts. I think I'm much better because of my first marriage, which was a struggle.

*　　　*　　　*

If I come home and I'm always more interested in playing baseball with my son than connecting with my wife, he's going to pick up on that and so will my daughter. And if he becomes my partner in a way, that's a lot of responsibility for a little tyke. And then they take that with them as they get older. We all pick up on some of that. That's some of how we grow up, but it happens more when there is a struggle between spouses and partners.

It's not their motivation. They pick up on it subconsciously.

87

It happened for a while in my first marriage. I would come home and there was that tension. What I used to do is have a conversation with my daughter. I just wasn't comfortable a lot of the time with my wife. Well, what happens subconsciously is she now takes on the role of supporting me in that way. Being my conversational partner in a way that really should be the spouse's role. That is a burden that a kid really shouldn't carry. And they're never going feel like they're doing well. They never feel like they can replace the mom or dad. We all get that to some extent. My mom was critical of my dad for not achieving. As smart as he was, he didn't achieve. What do you think happens to that voice? So now I have a freaking PhD. Why'd I do it? Probably because of my mom; I was filling that role. So being aware of that psychologically, I think it's important to have a good partnership. The family system revolves around that primary partnership. Sometimes you're the one that gets stretched because you have so many responsibilities as a father: a provider; come home you might be the baseball coach; might be a basketball coach; might take your daughter to a recital; whatever it is. The mother is doing different things during the day. Putting the energy into that primary relationship is something most people don't do. They take it for granted. So that's why I can't separate being a husband and being a father.

*　　*　　*

Our different styles are something that drove me nuts. One thing that helped is my work of understanding personalities. I did some work with my wife; but first I did some work with myself to understand my own personality and why I'm so friggin neurotic a lot of time before I started pointing to her neurosis. And that's helped us a lot; understanding how our different personalities drive us so much. Things that I did that drive her nuts far outweigh the things that she does to drive me nuts. She loves the kids as much as I do. I don't think she could love them any more. She's an incredible mom, but it's different.

*   *   *

My wife says I'm the play parent. She's the maintenance parent. The children seemingly have a more open relationship with me, according to her, because I'm not the one who has to do the disciplining. But it's really not the case. The kids talk to me in the car when we're all out. A lot of times, I'll come home, and they'll just say, *Code red, code red*, which is a warning to me that's she's in a bad mood.

*   *   *

When my wife is absorbed in a new past time that she enjoys, life gets better for the family. She taking a painting class now and it's occupying her, giving her something to think about. Life is much calmer. But then when she loses interest in that, I think it gets tough for her again. So we're always trying to find things for her to get involved with. I think she really loses perspective. For example, I don't know if you hear this, but I'm always hearing about how hard her life is. I'm always hearing how hard she has it. That she has to run the kids everywhere. She has to go shopping. She has to do this and that. It's always, *Poor me, poor me.* You can't say it, but you know what? I would trade with her in a heartbeat for a week. Because what she does in a week is what I do in about two days. It's her job. But again, it's because I think they lose perspective. So you get in the car and you drive around. What the hell else are you going to do? It's your job. It's not like if you're 15 minutes late for the soccer game, someone's going to fire you. Or there's some peer waiting to cut your legs out from under you. You got no pressure. You know what I mean, right?

*   *   *

I think we are a team in our roles. We haven't talked about it this way but I believe we have the same objectives for them. We

89

still have the same objective which is how you stay married. You at least have the same goals. You may differ on how to get there but you're not different on where you want to get to. So she loves her kids dearly. She just has a different way of dealing with them. Maybe the combination of our different approaches is what ultimately will help them make decisions as to how they want to raise their children should they have any. They're going to look at their parents and try to emulate those things they felt worked well for them and change or remove things that didn't work. That's all we can do.

*   *   *

It was kind of like the yin and the yang, the hard and the soft. But it wasn't something that we necessarily consciously decided upon or said, *I'm going to be this and you're going to be that.* We just kind of naturally slipped into those roles. She is more a homemaker, homebody type person and saw herself in the role of being supportive, and I saw myself as having to go out and hunt and kill and do what had to be done. It just kind of evolved that way. So it wasn't something that we had a whole lot of discussion about.

*   *   *

I think she knows I jump between roles. But it's also difficult on her sometimes. I'll give you an example. We were at my son's school for some kind of class presentation and he got to sit at our table. The teacher really likes my wife and so she sits between us. The teacher knows my son can get the work done and excel and is probably top of his class, but also knows there's a goofy side to him. She said, *I know where he gets it from.* And she tells my wife, *Look at those two. It's like those two are engaged. He's on his dad's every word.* My wife sees that and says, *Those two are just always together, always doing things.* So I think where I fall down a little bit is that I might be sometimes a little exclusive of her. I need to do a better job of including her when I'm playing the friend role and not the father, because when I'm playing father, she and I are synced up. But there's this other time when she wonders if she has two kids. But I don't think we've ever had a formal discussion around whose role is going to be what. I think we migrated naturally to roles that, hopefully, complement and not conflict.

*   *   *

I am still selfish as a person. I do like getting up early and doing my Starbucks thing on the weekend or going to the Eagles games or Flyers games. I've involved my son a lot more in those things. But where I could get better, I could involve his mom a lot more. I think she feels like too often it's me and him. I don't think I do as good a job as I could do with me, him and her together, the three of us.

*   *   *

My son has a great relationship with my wife which is special. That's the neat part about it. Not that I would want to change his relationship with her, or she would want to change the one he has with me. It's special and different. And that's what's really cool about it.

*   *   *

One of the hardest things was when our oldest was going through a tough time. I'd come home at the end of the day and almost literally open the door, lick my finger and stick the finger in to see which way the wind was blowing. I think one of the hardest things was that my wife and daughter would have had some blowup and I would walk in the door without knowing anything that happened. My wife would want my unanimous 100% support for whatever had happened and whatever decision was made. And my daughter would be looking at me wanting to tell me her side of the story. I don't know whether I ever got that one right. I would always say to my wife, *Look, can I at least hear what happened and what was going on before I say anything? I'm not going to question your judgment or what was happening but I can't even have an opinion unless I hear something about it.* For me to walk in the door and say, *Yeah, mom's right*, is very difficult.

Fortunately, that didn't go on all that often. I think we finally got to the point where if there was a disagreement, then the three of us could sit down. I was teaching philosophy in the 70s and 80s. There was a book called *Situational Ethics*. And one of the practices in there was called Rogerian Listening. It was a very interesting technique that I actually got my wife and daughter to use a little bit. Let's say you believe that McCain should be president and I believe that Obama should be president. And you know, we get involved in a political discussion. What Rogerian Listening demands is that you say, *Here are my reasons for why I think McCain would be a good president*. Before I can respond, *You're nuts*, I need to repeat back to you, to your satisfaction -- that's the key -- what your argument is. So before I can say, *I think you're crazy*, I need to say, *Well this is what I heard. I heard you say that McCain would be a good president for the following three reasons – boom, boom, boom*. And once you say, *Yes, you've heard me, that's right*, then I have permission to go ahead and say my piece. And without telling them, I got them to do that a little bit because I would say to my daughter, *Tell me what went on from your point of view* and, then say to my wife, *Before you say anything, let her report on what she heard. You may not think that she's right at all, but at least let her finish, and then you say your side, too.*

So each of them gave the other a chance to speak, even though they wouldn't have to necessarily do the full Rogerian thing. I had to be careful because one of the things my wife hated the most was if I treated the two of them the same. Boy did I fall on that one a number of times. But I think we made some progress in terms of being able to have one acknowledge to the other that at least she heard the other part of the story. I think that helped. But I will not claim that I figured that one out because in trying to manage my way through to have them understand each other, it made them feel that I was treating them like equals, and that really got my wife upset sometimes.

*　　*　　*

My son can respond differently to me than to my wife. I think sometimes there's a Y chromosome factor there, whether my voice is deeper or whether I'm still just physically bigger than he is or whatever, but he'll respond to me and get done what she wanted him to do. Later on, I can pull him aside and say, *Can we talk about what happened between you and Mom? Your mom asks you to do something four or five times and all you did was give her lip, and backtalk, as opposed to doing what you were asked. You know, you could have solved this long before my having to weigh in if you had just not been so feisty.*

*　　*　　*

My wife grew up without a father and with a mother who was an alcoholic and a drug user. So she really raised her two brothers and a sister. Her mother worked nights. During the day she literally slept the entire time. I give my wife a lot of credit because of her desire and her passion to be able to get out of her bad neighborhood, which none of her siblings has ever been able to do. She literally raised her three siblings and was able to get out. She paid for her way through college. She worked four jobs, literally, to be able to pay her tuition and to be able to have a little bit of pocket money and to be able to stay away from the horrible life that she had grown up in. As soon as she graduated from college she moved to New York to work and has never looked back.

93

And to her credit, she's done a good job in trying to help her siblings. Her one sister is a complete drug addict and disappears and re-shows up about once every other year. She's lived on the streets. We don't know what she's doing. My wife has helped her brothers get their lives together, although neither is doing that good of a job. We were able to get her mother to sell her row home, because the area just continues to go downhill, and move to an apartment complex which we helped her with. Her sister had a kid, no surprise, when she was 15 and she left home when she was about 18 or 19 and again was living on the streets for the last 5 or 6 years.

When we first started dating and got engaged, we had talked about what we wanted to do and how we wanted to live our lives. And both of us said how it would be awesome for me to be able to afford the opportunity to have her stay home and raise our children the way she wanted to be raised growing up. This could repair some of the damage that she suffered and make sure our children always had her at home. I think we've done a pretty good job.

You know how every neighborhood has a home that everyone goes to? That's what we've tried to build. That's what we've tried to instill in our children; that our doors are always open to any child in the neighborhood who wants to come in and play. We've got six of us but it's usually eight of us for dinner almost every night. Where one or two kids say, *Hey, can I come in for dinner?* We say, *Absolutely.* They go run and ask their parents. That's the type of environment she wanted to have, and she's taken her passion and her zest for corporate life and folded it into trying to being the best mom she can be. So we were on the same page when we talked about it, but financially we just weren't there initially and frankly weren't there when my daughter was born. Her schedule was just insane. Two of us were working crazy insane jobs. She was traveling all over the world. It just was never going to work. So, she gave up her career and we somehow got by financially. We are certainly doing better now.

*   *   *

Did I ever feel that raising kids wasn't enjoyable? Well sitting here, I would say, *No*, but I know there were times when we had our moments and not just one or two. I'm sure we had many when my stomach got tied up in a knot. Occasionally my wife and I yelled at each other about the kids. She still does. I really have learned over the years that this is love. But I just got to nod my head. She's yelling at me about the kids. It gets tiresome but I learned that there's no choice, I just have to listen to it. So did I ever feel differently? Yeah, but never to the extent of wanting to throw them out of the house or anything like that.

*   *   *

Some things we are in agreement on and some things we aren't. Over the years we were usually on the same page. And some things we still disagree on all together. It took a while but I think we've learned how to not cut the legs out from the other person if we disagreed. So things like the importance of school, the importance of family, the importance of responsibility in your life - - the core values I guess - - my wife and I are pretty much alike so we didn't even have to discuss these things.

On other things we differ. I tend to let the kids learn on their own. She's a lot more, *Do it this way. It's the right way to do it, so do it this way.* If the kids didn't make their bed, then they'd pay. I'd say, *Let's not make a big deal out of it*, but my wife is much more into the details of day to day life. If there was a family affair like a wedding, and if one of the kids wanted to stay at college, it was a major relationship crisis. And although I disagreed, I was more willing to say let them stay. I went through that phase. They're going through that phase.

95

But they are coming back and our family is very important. My kids are very close to each other which I really, really am glad about. They're very family oriented. They talk to their grandparents periodically on the phone and make every effort to do the family holidays. They call each other on their birthdays and they're very much into family vacations. I'm just tickled pink that they're very close to each other. My wife and I were at a conference with my daughter a couple of months ago and we took her out to lunch and she said she thinks her best friend in life is her brother. That's great.

* * *

I had believed you can make the kids do for themselves, but my wife believes that you just keep telling them. So at the end of the day my daughter wants new clothes. I said, *Well we're going to allot X amount of dollars for your clothing allowance. This is what we're going to spend on it. You want anything more, get it yourself. And when we spend that, then you can't have any more.* And when she comes and says she wants this new blouse or this new pair of jeans or whatever it is, and it's only July, I would say, *I'm sorry, the first six months you spent a whole year's allowance. If you want it, go get a job and buy it.* My wife believes you scream at her but at the end of the day you buy the damn jeans for her. I say, *No.* You don't scream at all. You just nod your head when she's frustrated and say, *If you get a job then you can pay for the jeans.* My wife screams at her and buys the jeans. I won't do that. And I think that's where they get the damn sense of entitlement.

* * *

This is my little victory because usually my wife takes the money and does what she wants to. My kids wanted cars. When they got their driver's licenses, I made the same deal with them. I said, *Get this grade point average, and get a job that will allow you to pay for your own gas and repairs, and I'll pay for the car.* A used car of course. The car and the insurance because they got a good grade point average. My second one, he just didn't care. He didn't want it that bad. He wasn't going to comply. He didn't get a car. My daughter, she complied. She got a car. She paid for her own gas and repairs. I bought the car and the insurance.

*   *   *

We have very much the same philosophy. And we grew up in very similar environments. My mother didn't work, her mother didn't work. We went to the same high school. We don't fight too much at all about philosophy. I think we had generally the same goals and objectives though we didn't plan them that way. I think they were probably instilled in us in terms of what we think is good and what we aspire to for our children. Same tactics? You know, I think our tactics may be complementary a little bit. We both spend a lot of time with them, but I think we bring different perspectives.

*   *   *

My wife is tougher on the kids in terms of expectations or in terms of grades. My wife is the classic lawyer. I'm the classic sales person. I'm trying to take the circular route to get there and she's like a bull in a china shop. So we both want the same thing, want to be successful. But if something needs to be done in 10 minutes, no matter what it is, she'll get it done in 10 minutes. But she'll leave a potential trail of destruction to get there, like take no prisoners. I think we're pretty good at figuring out who does what. I found out early in our marriage that it's tough to disagree. I'm not going to argue because she's trained to have arguments and I'm not. She sets a higher standard on that than I do. It's not that it's not important to me. I marvel at my kids and what they do in school. My 7th grader has more homework than I remember having in high school. Six hours of homework a night. Whether he gets an

A on a test or something else is fine with me. So I guess in general I'm more laid back and she's more the enforcer.

*   *   *

My wife has probably always been more of the nurturer. My son would probably approach my wife first, and then eventually would approach me. I think my one daughter would approach either my wife or me equally, and my other daughter would always approach my wife first. We're good together. As kids, we would always go to my mom if we wanted something. We would go to my dad if we really wanted to know something or if it was important. If it was something that was sort of menial, we would go to mom. Why bother dad?

*   *   *

I would say we didn't put our kids between us. We did not always agree, but the disagreement wouldn't be in front of the children.

*   *   *

I think to be honest, in terms of our approach to parenthood, we actually had on-the-job training like all parents. We were so young that we had to learn as we went along. There's been very little difference in the roles. We both are disciplinarians when we need to be. We have a really demonstrative family so we're both the nurturers as well. If the kids ever needed advice in terms of a career decision or when they had a problem with another person, they would tend to come to me. But if they had a relationship issue, they talk to their mother. But the difference there is very small because the reality is we would all talk very openly.

When we first had the kids, we agreed on a couple of things

98

right at the beginning. We're great negotiators with each other. We agreed on a couple of things. We wanted to learn from the good points and reject the bad points of each of our upbringings. We never allowed the kids to divide us. You know, the united front when kids try to manipulate a situation to their own advantage.

Communication was key for us. We're very open in how we communicate with the kids. Even now our 24 year old, if he oversteps the line, will get the reaming from hell from the two of us. And you know he's 24 and he's independent, but there's a line that you don't want to cross. So I think there were actually very small differences in our roles.

*　　*　　*

There's no question in my mind things go a lot better if the parents are on the same page. Your spouse needs to be on the same page with you, and if you're not, husband and wife need to go offline without the kids around. Talk about it and come up with some sensible resolution because the kids will exploit that. One of the things I noticed as a kid growing up was that if my mother was being really hard on me, my father would be somewhat understanding and comforting and vice versa. If my dad was coming down on me, my mother would actually show a softer side. I think it's good from the standpoint of young kids to have some sense of knowing that I can empathize with them, but I'm not undercutting what my wife is doing.

*　　*　　*

When we first got married, her mom was a stay-at-home mom. My mom was a stay-at-home mom. I think our desire going in was for that to be the case. We started out a little rougher than most. When I started working, unlike most of the staff who were single and footloose and fancy free and had no real responsibility, I had two kids and a wife.

I was 21 when my daughter was born, 22 when my son was born. You know, almost 23 and had a mortgage and a car payment and two kids and three mouths to feed besides mine. So in the beginning there really wasn't any question that she was going to stay home because we had two little ones. We always had the feeling that if I could make a certain amount of money, what would be the point of having somebody else raising our kids? We thought we needed a stable person who was always going to be there. So that when I was not, she was. If I had to travel, if I had to work late or whatever, she was the foundation.

*　　*　　*

I tend not to deal in absolutes for the most part. For me, not everything is black and white. With my wife, it's black and white, and on some level, that's a good thing. Like smoking pot. For my wife, if you're smoking pot, *No. Absolutely no.* My attitude is, *Look, you know it's illegal, right? You know if you get caught, you're going to get in trouble and you know it's not something you should really do.* But it doesn't make you the worst person in the world if you do it once or twice.

*　　*　　*

My kids are more likely to think of me as the more rational, reasonable parent and my wife as the more emotional, black and white one. I honestly think she has a stronger moral compass than I do. As much as I think I'm a good, decent, moral person, I think my wife is much more likely to be right down the line and not bend the rules anywhere, any way, shape or form. I just think some rules are not as important as others.

*　　*　　*

My wife is very supportive, very good and very generous to her kids. But they also know she doesn't support weakness and laziness and sloppiness. So as much as they know she's nurturing and a good mother, she also has high expectations. They clearly have a lot of love and respect for her.

*   *   *

We have different styles, which is good. My wife is somewhat like Mother Theresa. She wants everybody to get along and is not confrontational. In fact, she was always concerned that if I was too direct, that the kids wouldn't like me. And I said, *I'm not running a popularity contest.* If I were too rational when they were young, she would warn me they wouldn't like me. Well, I'll run that risk. But she was just as firm, interestingly enough.

*   *   *

I think the kids would probably say that I was more assertive, if you will. But she is enduring. I think when we were at our best, we spoke with actions. I can think of a time when my daughters were 12 or 13, you know, when mothers get stupid. Fathers, at 12, they get much smarter and mothers get kind of stupid. I think two stories sum it up. The first story, they were doing the, *Aw, mom,* and with the implication, *You are really as dumb as a box of rocks.* You tolerate a certain amount of that. That's part of their rite of passage. That's part of defining who they are. *I'm getting older, I'm getting smarter and therefore she must be getting stupider.* I got to the point where I understood it, but I was getting sick of condoning it.

We're in the kitchen. My daughters are doing the, *Aw, mom.* I'm sick of it. And I look at my daughters and I say, *You know girls, you're right. She really is a dumb shit.* Exact words. *She really is a dumb shit but when I decided to get married, she was the only one dumb enough to marry me.* My daughters got violent with me. My wife did not flinch. No facial expression, nothing. Didn't react at all. So she's the perfect foil. It's as if she

101

isn't there except she's four feet from me. And my daughters say, *Dad, you can't say that about mom.* I said, *What? I'm just agreeing with you. We don't keep secrets. I'm just agreeing with you. She's a dumb shit. That's what you are saying. You're not saying she's a dumb shit, girls, but the way you're acting, that's exactly what you're indicating. So what's your problem?* She was the perfect foil in that. She knew what I was doing. And she agreed with what I was doing.

About three weeks later, my wife had forgotten to take their blouses out of the dryer soon enough so they wouldn't be wrinkled, which is a heinous crime for a 12 or 13 year old. I mean the girls are really on her case. Dead calm. She said, *Please come with me.* Walks downstairs to the basement. *I'm going to say this once. This is the washing machine. Cold water only unless you want to have everything to come out pink or unless everything's white in the load. Don't put too much soap in. This is the dryer. I'm not capable of doing this to your satisfaction. Why don't you try it?* The twin 12 or 13 year olds went for three weeks doing their own laundry.

Then one day the girls came home from school. It was a Friday night. And this load of laundry was on their respective beds, done and folded. I've never heard so many *Thank you's* in my life. Actions spoke louder than words. She didn't get upset. She didn't say, D*on't treat me that way.* There wasn't a lot of verbiage around it. It was a non-verbal communication. Those are the cases when we were at our best, when I thought we were setting a good example.

*　　*　　*

I always took the, *Let them do it* philosophy or, *It's okay. Don't worry about it.* My wife and I would argue about it. My wife, she can be pretty hot headed and very pig headed. So we'd have a couple of arguments but mostly we agreed on that stuff. I think fundamentally we are in sync. So it never caused a real problem.

*   *   *

My wife is the patient one. The one who's with them all day long, and when I'm with them for a weekend, I wonder how she does it day in and day out, raising three boys. I respect her for that. When I'm with them, I try to be the dad who my dad was.

*   *   *

I married a materialistic woman who wanted everything now. I couldn't keep up with her demands for more money and more things even though I was working at one point on seven odd jobs, in addition to teaching. Our approaches to raising kids were very different. I wanted my kids to be involved in sports, church and cheerleading, and I wanted to be involved with them. But not my wife. She didn't want to spend money or time with the kids. And she resented my doing so.

*   *   *

My wife would use the kids as a wedge. She wanted to be the nice parent and tried to make me the disciplinarian. Reluctantly, I took on this role but I regret it. I had to travel a lot with work, and my wife told my kids I was away because I didn't want to be with them. She would go to their school when they were getting an award. I would go when there was a problem.

*   *   *

After we divorced, she would spend money on other things. She ran up huge credit card bills. She told the kids to hit me up for money for their activities. For four years, I lived in the basement of a row home. It had no heat. I hid this from the kids. At Christmas, I

103

took them to where I worked because there was a tree and more room.

* * *

When they got older I encouraged the kids to go to college. My wife was against it. Even though she remarried, she wanted the older kids to stay home and look after the younger ones. It took some doing, and a lot of borrowing and second jobs, but I got them through school.

I never bashed my wife in front of the kids. I always wanted them to feel they had two parents. I tried to shield them from my problems with my wife. I married a second time and my new wife liked my kids and vice versa. However, she and my first wife couldn't stand each other. My first wife did her best to ruin my second marriage.

* * *

I didn't want to be the guy who just sent the check. I stayed involved with my kids, part because I didn't trust my first wife to raise them, and part because I wanted them to be involved with sports, singing, and stuff with other kids and families – and not with drinking and drugs. I spent every weekend with them. I wanted to show good example. I loved them more than anything else. I wanted them to grow up and be successful.

Eventually, my one daughter couldn't stand my first wife and her new husband, so she moved in with me. Before long, my second wife got tired of the whole first marriage situation and not seeing me on weekends. We agreed to split amicably. I had warned her that I was fully committed to my kids.

* * *

My wife was an executive with a big company. But a couple years after the kids were born, she decided to stay at home. Our schedules were hard to coordinate and we decided that raising kids was too important to turn over to a nanny.

So we decided that she would quit work and stay at home until the youngest was 16. It was the best decision we ever made. The time goes so fast; you want to be there. No one is going to raise your kids better than you are. A million dollar nanny can't do as good as Mom and Dad. Would a nanny step in front of a bullet for your kids?

*   *   *

My wife and I tried to make decisions together. Sometimes her approach of, *Ask your father,* put me in a tough spot, but generally we were on the same page. My wife was always close to my daughters. They did a lot of things together when growing up. I was never as close to them as my wife is.

*   *   *

Kids are smart. They will play one parent against the other. We would call the kids on it when they did.

*   *   *

My kids would go to my wife with their problems. She is a better listener. I tend to analyze and provide solutions, but often kids don't want solutions. They just want someone to listen. My wife will listen for hours. She also gets in their face more. I am less confrontational.

*   *   *

My wife seems to be much more grounded than I am. She's

an incredible nurturer. She taught me what home was like. I didn't know. Now I do, and I think I can help create a home, but she really taught me that.

*   *   *

It's very interesting to watch my wife and me deal with an issue with the kids. If somebody gets her angry, she's on it. She will go right back at them. I tend to wait. I don't always get it right, but what I'm looking for is a moment where I can have a conversation where I feel like there might be ears to hear what I have to say. I've learned to say, *No,* or *No, we can't do that right now,* because sometimes you can't just wait. Sometimes you have to say, *No,* right in the heat of the battle. But I look to give reasons for why I say what I say. Oftentimes I may give a quick reason and then wait until later and I say, *Let's talk for a minute about what happened two hours ago or what happened yesterday.* Because I do feel that in order to move the peanut forward or make advances on it, there needs to be a time when discussion is possible, but discussion doesn't too often happen well in the heat of debate. Sometimes it's not good if you wait too long, but sometimes I feel that I can have more of an impact if I find a time when it seems like we're ready to have the conversation.

*   *   *

My wife and I have similar philosophies of child raising. We both want to see well rounded kids who can have good relationships with men and women. Hopefully go on to lead an adult life of their choosing. I think one of the things that we do differ on is, when do you transition from command and control to coach? I think I transition earlier than she does. Remember, I spent years as an athletic coach, so I have a different grounding and orientation. I probably apply those principles earlier in the game. I'm not saying I had it right or wrong but I do see that there's a point where the command, *Do this cause I'm your mother,* begins

106

to lose its impact. I probably shifted away from that approach earlier.

* * *

I believe the children have a much better relationship with me than they do with their mother. We have a much better relationship. Mom will say it's because I am the "play parent" and she's the "maintenance parent." Not really true. It's the way we deal with them. I deal with the kids very objectively, so even when I'm angry with them, they'll almost always agree there's a good reason for me to be angry. I don't fly off the handle for no reason, whereas mom tends to be more emotional. Some small thing may set her off. They're not stupid. These kids know when mom's overboard. I don't do that with them. I express my displeasure. I explain why, if they don't already get it. And they typically will say, *You're right dad. I screwed up*, and I move on. Whereas mom will continue harping on them and that just doesn't do any good after a while. So I've learned with these kids, especially the boy, you make sure he gets the message and then you move on. So we have a good relationship. They talk to me. Both kids speak to me openly about things they probably don't talk to their mother about.

* * *

Wives and Mothers

Questions:

1 *Are your roles different from your spouse's? How so? Are you*

 both comfortable with these differences in roles? Are these

107

differences productive in raising the kids, or are they a hindrance?

2 *Have you and your spouse discussed what you want for your kids, what you want them to become, and how you should raise them?*

3 *In terms of raising the kids with your spouse, are you both on the same page and working in the same direction, or are you at odds with each other?*

4 *If you are at odds, is there something you can improve upon? How?*

Values

Kids need to understand values, but they learn these from example. You also need to tell them when they are wrong.

I don't believe in taking half way measures, so I try to instill that in them.

I think my approach to being a father is a combination of emulating the things I thought my father did that were great and trying to introduce things that I wish he would have done.

Work hard and play by the rules.

I think my wife and I are trying to be role models. I think my kids would basically say they went through life without too much trauma. We had some, but they grew up in a stable household. It was important for me to provide financially; they both were able to go to college and graduate school and they owed no debt. That was something that I wanted to do. I was able to do it. But I don't think it hurts for a kid to struggle a little bit.

*   *   *

There are basic things that every child needs. The ability to love and care about people is one of the core attributes that I proudly talk about. Trying to summarize what I think are the greatest values of my five children? They truly appreciate other people. They value them. They have the ability to be open-minded and understand that people are different, and I think it allows them to be more comfortable as human beings. It allows them to fit in more easily in whatever setting they are in. And they don't seem to have the prejudices that, unfortunately, the generation before me had. Now I don't know if that's societal or it's parental, but after a while I think parenting is what produces societal values.

*   *   *

We have a very open, democratic house. Everyone has a say. It's everyone's house. But the parents break the tie when necessary.

*   *   *

I remember bugging my daughter about how much money as a waitress she was making. She got tired of it. She said, *Dad, do I ask how much money you make?* I got my tax return that night and left it out for her to see, with a note that said, *This is for us, not for outside the family.* She gave it back with a note: *I made $280.00 last night.*

*   *   *

I want our children to be open to accepting new ideas, not necessarily embracing them but open to understand them and to at least evaluate them. I think that's healthy. I think the responsibility of a parent is not to close, which is what a lot of parents do, close that opportunity. Parents, if they instill too strong a position, limit their children's ability to grow. I see that a lot. I find it difficult when I see young people having such strong opinions that are narrow in scope. I love to hear them suggest, *Well, let's talk about it*, and they're open to having a dialogue. I think caring and loving, to know that that they have responsibilities to themselves and the people they love, and a greater responsibility to the human good, are things that a parent needs to instill.

*   *   *

I made manager when I was 27 and about two years later I had my first child. I tried at that point to get people at work to accept that I was leaving at 6:00 no matter what. The hours from 6:00 to 9:00 were sacred. Over time, all my clients knew about it. I let people in the office know about it. I said I'm available but just not for three hours of the day. And I found that that commitment created a vehicle for communication with my kids that's irreplaceable. There's something about a daily meal together after school or after work. Where even if not much is said, it was the opportunity for someone to say something about what's going on in school if they didn't understand what they were dealing with. I would say that at some of those dinners, maybe a third of them, I was exhausted and zombied out, but I don't think it mattered. I think just being there and having this sort of anchor in the kids' lives was key. As I got older, we didn't have dinner at 6 -- it became 6:30 then 7, then 7:30. But I would say out of 20 dinner nights Monday through Friday, if we missed four of those, that would be a lot.

*   *   *

I didn't do client dinners. I didn't do that stuff. I just didn't do it. My kids had after school activities but they were home by 6 or 6:30. And that's what we did. And then you hang around after dinner in case there are homework issues.

*   *   *

111

I have played bridge once a month for the last 22 years with the same guys. The third Friday of every month we play cards. We never missed. If somebody had to miss, we had a back up. There are five of us. Some of those other four fathers, who were probably the most aware of issues with their kids, separately pulled me aside maybe seven years apart. They said basically the same thing. *I think the reason your kids turned out better than ours is that I didn't spend any time with them. I was never home.* Some of their kids went a bit astray. Not in big ways but they just don't have quite the motivation and direction that maybe comes if you're a more involved kind of father. I don't put a lot of pressure on my kids. Maybe the other fathers figure I did.

*   *   *

Let me tell you about the vacation thing. Everyone at work knew about this and I probably handed out my vacation itineraries to 50 professionals in this town over the last 15 years. I did it for seven years in a row because you only have a five to seven year window when your children mind you, when they're old enough to appreciate it, get something out of it, but not so old that they don't want to be with you.

So to me, that window is like from ages 8 to 15. Below 8, you can go to Disney World anytime, but below 8, they're not going to get much out of it, and above 15, they really don't want to be with you. We did these trips, seven summers in a row, for two to three weeks in length. They had a combination of fun, which you couldn't experience during the rest of the year, and educational content. They were all done exactly the same way. I would spend close to a year planning the itinerary because if you want to go to the Ahwahnee Lodge in Yosemite, you have to book that a year in advance. If you want to take the narrow gauge railroad from Durango, Colorado to Silverton, Colorado, you have to book it a year in advance. And by booking it a year in advance, that becomes the center point of your vacation and you're sort of under the gun to build around it.

These trips were all the same. I have a big cooler. I put my kids' pillows from home in the cooler and checked it in as a piece of luggage. I'd rent a van and the van had to have two benches in it. I didn't want seats. I wanted them to be able to sleep in the van if they had to with their pillows. So each had a bench. My wife and I were up front. We had an itinerary to explore a 300-mile circle around that part of the country. Always built around national parks. Not camping out. We never really roughed it. We always had a fishing day, a white water rafting day, a hiking day and it also had things you do with the rangers in the park. These were phenomenal trips. You can get these passports from the national park service, and they stamp them. The kids, when they were younger, were really into it. National parks are phenomenal attractions in this country.

We had a ball. We built trips around northern California, southern California, Arizona, southern Utah, Wyoming, Mt. Rushmore, and Glacier National Park. These were phenomenal, inexpensive trips. And they weren't frivolous. My wife said what was great about the trips was all the driving in the van because that's when you could really bond with your kids and talk to your kids and sort of get into it. Perhaps for 50 miles no one said a word. Other times, we'd be sharing the experiences of the day before or that morning or something funny. In the morning, we'd buy lunch for the day and put drinks in the cooler. Just being in a van, all self contained like that, was great. I'm still doing it to a much different degree. Recently, I got my kids together, even at their ages. No girlfriends or boyfriends. We went to Norway, Sweden and Denmark.

*   *   *

Kids need to understand values, but they learn these from example. You also need to tell them when they are wrong.

113

*   *   *

To know right from wrong. To know that there is something beyond them, that they need to be able to have a positive influence upon others. To know the importance of family and the importance of community. The importance of education.

Religion? It depends how you define religion. To me, religion is a core value, that's number 1. In my case, being Jewish, it is also a cultural connection I would like them to have, and it's a spiritual component that helps them through perhaps some difficult times. But it's not a dogma. We're going through some interesting things on the religion side with my kids. But it's mostly about core values.

*   *   *

Important is to make sure they're happy, well adjusted, productive people and have an impact on the world. They're not worrying about paying their way through college so they have the ability to do other things.

*   *   *

You look at material possessions growing up in a town like this. There are a lot of rich kids around. A lot of the rich kids flaunt, and a lot of the parents flaunt, the money that they have. My daughter is 15, not driving yet, and tells a story of a girl in her class, also 15, not driving yet, who has not one car but two cars. My kids have begun to recoil from that. To say things like, *I hate living here. I hate these kids.* It's hyperbole and they exaggerate sometimes, but they have recoiled from the unbridled manifestation of wealth. They're repulsed by it to the point where one daughter is saying, *Take the SUV and drop me off. Don't take the Lexus. I don't want kids to know I'm like them.* It's interesting. A dilemma I have is how to teach them about money and

114

managing it, without over-emphasizing its importance in a way that will be a turnoff.

*   *   *

I think most of us have failed more than succeeded on a point-by-point basis when it comes to being a parent, but on the overall, we've mostly succeeded. Maybe that's extreme, but if you took every single transaction, every interaction, every thought and you added them all up, I would say more have failed than passed. Meaning that I'm doubting myself on this particular decision. Or I yelled at my kid, or I said *No* when I should have said *Yes*, or said *Yes* when I should have said *No*, or I didn't see this happening or didn't spend enough time with him. If you add it all together, somehow it becomes a pass. It's a hell of a test. It's hard enough for us to really raise ourselves. What do we want for ourselves midlife? You talk about reaching your potential, making sure you take advantage of every opportunity that you have, being happy, accepting yourself. Now you're trying to do that for your kids, too. We can't even do it for ourselves.

*   *   *

Well, originally, we had our first. My wife kept working at least part time just to help make ends meet. When the second was born, we realized with two kids, we wanted them to have this stability of mom being home or one of the parents being home all the time. Because that's the way I had it. I had a mother growing up and it was real important for me in terms of having an anchor in the home. Someone I could count on always being there for me. Especially when I was young. Kids are babies. That's when they're being shaped. I don't want them being shaped by a stranger. If I couldn't afford to not have her work, or we couldn't afford to not have her income, then we'd do what we had to. Nothing against that. But, we were willing to suck it up a little bit in the early years, when we had two kids and lived on one income. We both felt it

115

was important to have a mom at home.

*   *   *

I am a very loving father, but I'm also a very demanding father. I'll put it in that order because I'm fairly tough on them relative to things that I believe are important. Things I believe are important are that they're good human beings, they're good people, that they treat people the way they like to be treated. In other words, treat everyone with respect. I expect them to excel at everything they do. And excel means do the best they can. I don't believe in halfway measures. So that's sometimes hard on them. If you're going to do it, do it to the best of your ability or don't bother doing it. That applies to school, social life, personal, whatever it is. I don't believe in taking half way measures so I try to instill that in them.

*   *   *

You know what I want these kids to do? I want them to be happy. I'm in a profession. I can't profess to love my profession. I certainly don't dislike it. There are aspects that I really enjoy. But is this my passion in life? No, it's not. I got into this business because I was graduating college. I needed to get a job and make money. I would like for my children to be able to pick a profession that they really enjoy, that they can make their life's passion, outside of their family. I'd like them to pick a profession where they make a reasonable living but I don't want them to have to pick it based on primarily how much money they could make. So one of our goals is to leave them enough money such that they never have to worry about it.

*   *   *

I think my approach to being a father is a combination of emulating the things I thought my father did that were great and

116

trying to introduce things that I wish he would have done. One thing my dad was really great at was being clear on expectations. He was pretty strict about making sure those expectations were not only clearly understood, but followed. But at the same time, he provided everything I needed to succeed. At least the physical. My dad wasn't outwardly demonstrative, so I try to do that more with my kids. My dad rarely talked to me. If anything, he talked at me. So I try out conversations with my kids and they're pretty open with me about things. I can even get the boy to talk to me about girls sometimes. There are things I think we could do better, but I don't think we're doing a bad job. I think these kids are going to grow up to be good people. I think they'll be able to take care of themselves. That's all you can really ask for.

*   *   *

I was never interested in trying to position myself in the right way with the right people. My wife got a gift for helping out in school one day. She got a coffee mug and a $10 gift card. And my son said that the school teacher must be poor because she only gave a modest gift card. I go, *What does that have to do with anything, if she has money or doesn't have money? It was a gift.* I have some basic beliefs. That is one of them. I am friends with a guy that ran the copy machines. I like the guy who pushed the mailroom cart around, too. Some other friends are doing pretty well in business but I just don't see much of a difference about the house they have and the car they drive. Are they fun to hang out with? Do I have a good time with them? Do I like talking to them? Do I like being around them? But, I can see that one coming up on my son's radar screen. Somebody has money and somebody doesn't have money. I stopped him in his tracks and said it shouldn't matter at all. I should maybe explore that a little bit more.

*   *   *

I know this guy who has five kids. They all went through Yale and that was important for him, to get his kids through Yale. But the killer sentence there is: it was important to him. He got his kids through Yale, but who knows what's truly important to his kids? I'm not there yet with my son but I think I'm giving him enough of a platform to figure out what those things are, and the opportunity to choose. We'll see. I just hope he makes good decisions.

*   *   *

I think one aspect of where I could be better is practicing my faith. I was brought up Catholic, still am Catholic. I have lived my life by those principles but I don't practice it enough. My wife is the one that practices the Catholic faith in our household. She goes to church every Sunday. But now my son's watching me and I'm sitting home or doing something on the lawn while she goes to church, and he's hanging out with me on the sideline. I need to work on it. It's an easy thing to work on, and there's no reason to not work on it other than just being lazy. I wonder about the downstream effect of that laziness. I know being lazy in other parts of my life can rub off on him. I really do guard myself about being lazy in other aspects. I just won't go home and watch TV and be lazy there. I get up early every morning on Saturdays.

*   *   *

I try and do a lot of the stuff that my dad didn't do. I'm real passionate about being with my kids. I try and do the work/life balance as best I can. When I come home from work, I really try to shut off and forget the office. I'm home as much as I can possibly be home. To bathe the kids, to play with the kids, to have dinner with the kids, to help out with the homework. To just be there and be out on the front lawn joking with all the neighborhood kids and having fun and playing. And I never saw that in my father. And I really make an effort to make sure that I do that because that's why

118

you have children. You have children to have fun, and if you're not going to do the things that need to get done with kids, why even bother?

We kids grew up at the Knights of Columbus bar. We'd sit in the booth and people would be smoking all over the place, and my dad would throw a couple of quarters at us for the vending machine to get a soda. I don't want my kids to even be in bars as a result of that. Whatever my kids get involved in or interested in, I always try and do it too. I don't think my father had ever done that. I just think that that's my responsibility; that's my job and frankly, it's fun. And the relationship I have with my kids as a result of it is great. When I come home and walk in the door, they basically tackle me like Fred Flintstone's dog tackled him.

*   *   *

And it's just the greatest feeling in the world. I get this proposal at work which is a complete disaster. I had a horrible day yesterday. I was at the Phillies game entertaining clients, and my phone was ringing off the hook. It was just a train wreck of a day. And I remember pulling down my street and there are two of my kids outside doing whatever the hell they're doing. They were jumping up and down when I got out of the car and were tackling me and giving me kisses and hugs. That just kind of puts it all in perspective. And then they go to bed around 8:30 or 9:00 at night, and I'm back online cracking away until 11:00, 12:00, 1:00 in the morning. But at least I had that time to break away and realize that's why I do what I do. And that's pretty powerful. My father just never did that. I look back and I think how sad that is because he just didn't have the relationship that he should have had with us.

*   *   *

I'm very close to all of the other neighborhood kids because they spend a ton of time at our house. It's amazing. My wife and I talk about some of the dads in our cul-de-sac. They couldn't care less. They couldn't care less about their kids. This one girl spends more time at our house than she probably does at her own home. Her mother doesn't care. Her father's never home and doesn't care at all about her. I see her getting more attached to me and wanting to joke and have fun and just be crazy. And that's what I try to do with our kids; throwing them up in the air; bouncing on the trampoline; swinging on the swing set; playing tag with them; teaching them how to golf; taking them to the pool; all that basic kind of blocking and tackling stuff of having fun. We always want everyone at our house. I have fun with all my kids' friends. I interact with all their friends, and it's just an awesome feeling because you see how much the kids really like to laugh and giggle. It creates that atmosphere that my wife and I really wanted to create.

*   *   *

I always reflect back on my father and the lack of interface that I had with him that I wish I would have had. I just didn't, and I think that it's critical to me to be able to make sure that the kids have that ability in me. I would never come to my father and say, *I just broke up with this girl. This girl just dumped me.* I never had that ability to open up. On anything. I never, ever, ever, ever want that for my children.

*   *   *

I think it's so critically important to be involved. It goes so quickly. My oldest is in college. I remember my holding him when he was a little baby. I wake up and he's graduated high school.

*   *   *

I've got four sayings that I live by. 1. Today is a gift, that's why they call it the present. 2. Excelling at home is more important. 3. Life is 10% of what happens to you and 90% how you react. 4. The answer's always *No* if you don't ask the question. And I try and look at these four quotes every single day before I start my work day. I try every morning. That's what helps me get motivated and keeps me energized. Just these four quotes. That's just part of who I am. I try and live those types of values. I said to my friends, *You got to take care of your home life, because if you're home life's good, you can manage everything else. Take care of home life and home life will take care of everything else.*

*   *   *

If someone came in our house at certain times of the week, they'd think, *My God. What the hell are you doing?* There are toys all over the place. There's a diaper here that's dirty and the dishes are piling up. I always say to my wife, *You know, so our house looks like shit. So what? What do we care? In five or ten years from now when the kids are all out doing their thing, we'll have an immaculate house and we'll take care of it then. But why bother? Like, who cares?*

We used to kill ourselves. Like at 11:30, 12:00 putting every toy back where it's supposed to go. One night, probably three years ago, we just looked at ourselves and said, *What the hell are we doing?* Like who cares? Are the kids sloppy a little bit? Probably more so than they should. I don't do dishes when the kids are around. Who cares? We'll run the dishwasher when we can run the dishwasher. If we're out of food, we'll go out to grab dinner or something.

What we're really trying to do is just say, *Stop. Stop with the routines and get out and live.* And that's what we're really trying to do. I make Target runs on Saturday mornings. I bring all four kids and we have cart races. I say to my daughter, *We need this; go get it.* She'll run through the store. Make it a game. Get the wrong stuff and who cares? We'll throw it in there and my wife will yell at me because I come home with all sorts of shit we didn't have on the list. But I try and make it fun. I never did that as a kid. And they love it. They laugh. They have cart races themselves and they're hanging on the sides and falling off and getting hurt and jumping back on. I never did that before. I just try and make everything fun. I don't think we do enough of that. Now we're starting to get out and do more in the neighborhood. We're saying *Yes* to the neighbors inviting us over, whereas before, aw Christ you know. My wife would say, *I haven't showered in two days because of the kids* and this and that. I said, *Throw a goddamned baseball hat on and put on some makeup and let's just go.* Like who cares? Who really cares? And we're starting to do a lot more of that.

*   *   *

The one saying that came out of a book, which I think was so simple and so true was, *Work hard and play by the rules.* And I tell the kids that all of the time. Sometimes they know I'm going to say it. But I think that's pretty important. If you decide to be an engineer, professional baseball player, musician, work at Wawa, whatever it might be, work hard and play by the rules. I think you'll be happy and then you can define success the way you want to define success. A lot of the time success gets defined for you, but I think you've got to define success for yourself. Certain values you want to pass along to them. But I think that you've also got to give them the autonomy to do things on their own, to do the things that are of interest to them. Be supportive in that and let them make mistakes. That's really the only way they'll learn. If your parents fight all your battles and don't allow you to make some mistakes, I think you'll become too dependent on them. As much as all that's comforting, I think it's not in their best interest longer term.

*   *   *

122

Determine what you should hold back and not let your kids do or get. We're fortunate enough that we can provide them a lot of material things. They're good kids and they do well in school and they're generally respectful and all that. You want to give them stuff, but you want them to appreciate what they get as well. I know I was very fortunate growing up that we didn't want for anything. Our parents didn't give us too many things. I know my dad was in a family of six kids. He put himself through college. He was the first one in his family to go to college. He didn't really get any help from home. They weren't in a position to help him. He took public transportation to college. He took public transportation back and forth to work. He worked very hard. He had a work ethic that rubbed off on us even though we didn't observe it all because a lot of that was done before any of us was born. We really didn't fully know what he and my mom sacrificed. That's a challenging thing that my wife and I often talk about. You want them to have everything but you don't want them to have too much, and drawing that line is hard. I don't think they have complete appreciation for how fortunate they are.

*   *   *

My wife is great at getting the kids to thank others. Writing thank you cards all the time. She is much more task oriented and efficient than I. If we go somewhere and get something, when we come home, she won't go to bed without writing thank you cards. She's forced the kids to sit down and write cards in their own handwriting. When my daughter graduated from eighth grade, she sent a thank you card to every teacher she had in the eight years that she was there. And it's amazing. The teachers came back to my wife. They knew that she made my daughter write it and said, *I'll never throw that away*. I don't think people get thanked as much as we think they might get thanked. And I give my wife all the credit for that because she's very persistent and she never lets an opportunity go by for them not to, in writing, thank somebody. After practice or a game we always remind them, *Go up and say thanks to the coach because they put a lot of time in.*

*　　*　　*

I would like to describe my kids as good people who are happy. And that they use all of their talents.

*　　*　　*

Happy people are said to have two traits: health and empathy. You know, the ability to put yourself in someone else's shoes and show self awareness. I urge my kids to be empathetic and put themselves in someone else's shoes. You can always be more aware of where you are in circumstances, when you should say something and when you shouldn't say something, and what might hurt or offend somebody. My wife and I remind them of being self aware and being empathetic because it's easy to take a stance against somebody, but if you can step back and at least know where they're coming from, you may still disagree but you don't take certain things personally. I try to apply this myself because I'm not always the most empathetic and not always the most self aware.

*　　*　　*

I think the biggest challenge as a father is how much to give your child and when to hold back, and when to push and not to push. Sometimes you like to think the best course of action for your child is to do x, but maybe you got to let them find their way. And it's so challenging because you want them to have everything. You want them to be successful. You want them to be happy. You want them to have this experience and that experience. You want what's good for them, but how they need to get to that place is sometimes different. When they're smaller, there's not a lot of autonomy there. It's when to push and when not to push; when to let them go down their own path to pursue something. Maybe you

124

think they should go soft left and they want to go hard left, or soft right or they want to go hard right. I think you've got to give them some rope. As they get older I think that's more challenging to do.

*   *   *

I've often said parents fail in a couple of ways. One, when they're too controlling with their kids. Tightly controlled; telling them what to do; dictatorial almost. But then you have those that are not controlling enough, not involved enough, not vocal enough. Trying to be their friends. It's that balance. We know there's a balance somewhere, but where exactly is it?

*   *   *

We know we're going to get it wrong sometimes. If you're batting over 500 you're probably doing okay.

*   *   *

I remember the phrase *Time is love*. I certainly believe that. I believe spending time with your kids, doing things, even simple things is really important. One thing that we've done that was different than our parents is carving out family time, quantity time. We eat together as much as we can; have meals together as opposed to everybody eating on their own. We'll do a game one night a week or a movie night or something to just stay connected, and that's been fun. The down side is probably we don't get out enough, the two of us, but we do a lot as a family. Later on, but we'll have plenty of time for that.

*   *   *

How do you build a person? There's a book that I read a long time ago called *People Making*. How do you mold a child? It's structure, discipline and delaying gratification. And I used that

125

as an operating model for how I relate to my kids. It means knowing right from wrong, liking yourself, having confidence enough in yourself that you're not following the crowd. You always follow the crowd a little bit, but you need a compass to help you along the way. Hopefully, you've got a relationship with your siblings and with your parents that will help you.

*　　*　　*

I didn't let my work compromise my family. I would work ungodly hours but I'd go home at 3:00 to be coaching because 3:30 is game time. I made sacrifices so that I could always be available, and I think my kids knew that I would always be there. They weren't all star athletes either. Most fathers or mothers would drop them off and told them to find their own ride home or something. My kids never had to worry about getting to places or if someone would be there to pick them up.

*　　*　　*

We have a very strong rule…women are to be respected and if anyone touches a woman, it doesn't matter what you need to do, you do it. Whether it be your sister, your mother, your daughter, your girlfriend, your friends; if anybody touches a woman, hell hath no fury. Another rule, support each other. Don't put the family second. That's my mom's Italian influence in growing up in Southside Chicago. Don't ever put the family second and expect there not to be consequences. You can, but there are absolute consequences if you pick friends over family. The general rule was take care of the family, take care of each other, and today my kids look out for each other.

*　　*　　*

If you do all the little things right along the way, the big things in life will take care of themselves. Small and large is sort of

126

a process. If you open the door, if you hold the door for somebody, if you use good manners, you say, *Thank you.* Just happened the other day. I was down the shore. The person waiting our table, I asked her what her name was. She said, *Well thank you for asking.* To me, to know someone's name is important. She was tremendously polite and I thought it was great. That to me is an example of doing something small. Treat people the way you like to be treated. I think doing all those little things becomes the DNA of your whole personal outlook, your family outlook, your professional outlook. If you can take care of all those things along the way, then there's not a lot that you have to worry about in the big score sheet of what went right, what went wrong. More things will go right. They won't all go right but you have a better chance.

*　　　*　　　*

I would say the comfort of family in good times and in bad is very important to health and well being. I think being able to take refuge in your family when you need refuge, and provide refuge when they need refuge, is a very important thing from the standpoint of living a healthy life. And the importance of friends which is a natural extension of our family. We have very good friends that are lifelong friends. And we can call on them in an instant and without asking a question. You need something, they don't ask questions. It's nice to have people like that in your life.

*　　　*　　　*

Did the kids pull away from us because it wasn't cool to hang out with their parents? No. Actually, they didn't get into as much trouble as other kids because we had such a strong family. They would have as much fun going to the movies with us as going out drinking with their friends. Or overnight. They didn't all run someplace on the weekends to get an outlet. They didn't feel they had to run someplace to grow up. It wasn't a controlled environment. They could take risks. I let the kids drink. I had four

17 year olds that are going into college in six months. They could come and have a sleepover at our house and play beer pong in the basement. So I think you have to create enough of an opportunity for them to take risks so that they learn they have limits and know where those limits are.

*   *   *

I think I am a disciplinarian but it was an early discipline. You have something with the "ultimate no" without being physical. You want to have a way to be able to get to their souls and say there are things that you just shouldn't do. I could do it verbally because it was sort of drilled into them from an early age that kids should behave. You should be quiet when you're out in company. If you're at a restaurant, you're there to eat, you're not there to cry. Sure our kids probably did their share of crying but they didn't do a lot of it. The evidence was even when they were young, they would always be welcomed to be with us if we had friends over the house. We didn't hide the kids or have them scurry away. We never had an au pair. We had babysitters but the babysitters were usually college age kids who were fun to be around. We didn't take a lot of trips where we left them with people. We didn't have a lot of relatives to leave them with, but most of our relatives I wouldn't leave my kids with anyway. We didn't feel the need to always escape from our kids. We enjoyed being with our kids and I think they enjoyed being with us.

The hard thing in all of that is that because it was such a strong environment, it's hard for them to make friends, adult friends. I think you always need to have one very good friend. You need a best friend, and in different ways each of our kids had a little difficulty with getting that best friend. Maybe that's one thing I would have liked to have done different, to create a little more separation so that they could have that best friend to confide in where it wasn't mom or dad.

*   *   *

Taking kids to where you're working, or doing volunteerism or community outreach that your kids can participate in, is tremendous. They see you in a different light than your home role. The worse thing that I could imagine is if your only perception of your father is the guy who left in the morning, came home late at night, and never saw you beyond that.

*   *   *

I think the image that kids get a lot today about what it means to be a man is just totally off base. You know, this kind of macho stuff, controlling, not showing emotion. To me that's the furthest thing from the truth. I think you can be strong without being controlling. I think you can be a force in the family and still show your emotional side. I think that that allows kids to identify with you much more so than the fatherly figure that never shows any emotion. That's just not real.

A lot of what I do with my kids is what I do in relationships with just about anybody. I think you need to be genuine. I think you need to be honest. I think you need to take responsibility for what you say and do. I definitely think you need to have high expectations for yourself and those who you're dealing with, be it at work or at home. And I also think you need to be willing to recognize your mistakes, and own up to them because nobody's perfect as much as you try to do the right thing. And I think if you do those things, you'll also be able to empathize better.

*   *   *

I think you've got to be engaged in your kids' lives, but it can be tough depending on what your job is. It's vitally important that you make time for your kids. With my dad working as hard as he did, and he had a second job for a portion of the time when I was growing up, he didn't coach my little league baseball team and he rarely went to a game. He was either working a second job on

Saturdays at my uncle's machine shop or he was doing stuff around the house because we didn't hire contractors to come in and do stuff. I think he regretted not having that opportunity to do more.

* * *

What I'm starting to see with my kids is that it's important to try to have individual time with them as well as joint time because I think any kid likes to have undivided attention with a parent. I don't know if we do a good enough job of that, but it's something that we're trying to stay focused on.

* * *

I did a lot of traveling early in my career. I was away three of four nights a week. My first boss was one of the nicest men I ever knew and he took me under his wing. His advice to me: *Call home every night, wherever you are, and talk with your wife and kids.* I followed his advice. Every night. The nightly talks went on until the kids went off to college. But even then, we talked about four times a week. Weekends were all about the kids, not about golf. I was a coach for a lot of their sports, and when I wasn't a coach, I still went to every game.

* * *

I tried to give my kids a strong work ethic. I tried to teach them how to treat people respectfully and be responsible young adults. I am proud of them.

* * *

Education has always been important to me. My grandmother used to say, *They can't take it away from you.* However, my kids never really inherited my focus on education.

130

Only one of my four was a natural student.

*   *   *

I worked hard but was not a workaholic. I never missed a birthday. I would leave work early and pick up the kids. I would do my share of laundry, diapers, bathing, etc. I tried to continue this when the kids were away at college. Visiting them. Taking them and their friends out to dinner. I developed a close relationship with them early. Lincoln logs and board games when they were little; golf and trips when they grew up.

*   *   *

I tried to spend as much time as I could with the kids. I remember driving home one night from out of town. It took me three and a half hours - - to hear one of the kids play *Ode to Joy* in an orchestra for three minutes at a school concert. Then I drove back that night for a morning meeting.

*   *   *

I wanted to guide and influence my kids. This required me to be there with them. I wanted to know and spend time with them. I wanted to know and spend time with their friends. Still, there are so many influences on them. You do the best you can, and then hope for the best. You hope your values take hold: honesty, charity, responsibility, love of family, hard work. It helps if they saw you live by these values, instead of just talking about them.

*   *   *

My wife and I once asked the kids what they would have wanted us to change or not change. Two things they didn't want us to change. One was we spent a lot of time with them and they really liked that. We took vacations together. We did all that stuff.

131

Only one time when they were growing up did my wife and I ever go on a vacation by ourselves. It was nice but that was the only time we ever did that. The other thing they commented on was that they never had to guess about where I stood on something. So even though they may have chosen to do something that we didn't like, they were fully aware that we weren't going to approve. So there was no ambiguity about the decisions they had to make and whether or not we would approve. They knew exactly where we were and they said retrospectively they appreciated that.

*   *   *

I think if I stayed, I could have been president of the bank. But I made a decision to forsake some of the career path because of the balance of the family. Right or wrong, it's the way I chose to live. I was always at my kids' activities. My kids played athletics in high school. I tried to get to every game. My youngest daughter played two sports at college. I tried to get to them as much as I could.

*   *   *

Values

Questions:

1   *What do you value most in life? Do these differ from your spouse's?*

2   *What values do you most want for your kids to learn and live?*

3   *How are you teaching and reinforcing these values?*

4   *Does how you are leading your life reinforce these values? Conflict with them?*

5   *Do you need to change anything? Will you? How?*

Kids...Different Kids

*Each child is different. Some children will cry out loud,
others will cry inside.*

*My girls were easier to raise than my boys. The girls were
more focused, more organized, more ambitious and more mature
at the same age.*

*Girls are tough because they hold grudges. Guys, you kick
them in the ass and that's it.*

*The goal should be to get to know each kid as a person, not
just as your child.*

Did one get more attention than the other did? Did one get
more attention because she was a better athlete than the other? It's
hard to assess when you're doing it.

*   *   *

I think raising children is a personal thing. I don't believe that there's one way of raising kids. I think each child is different and each child needs a different kind of attention...different kind of love. I don't believe in this concept that everything is equal. Every child should be treated differently. Everything in life should be that way. You could love differently and it's the same quantity of love, but it's just different for each child. It's a little tricky when you have multiple children because they make a lot of comparisons. They want to know why one gets one thing and one doesn't get the other.

*   *   *

I think you learn from children. I have the advantage of having five kids. Three of my own, and two I inherited. All five are distinctly different, unique personalities. All of them come to the table with different intellectual skills, people skills, everything -- and how I relate to each one of them is different.

*   *   *

My kids started out in public school. I'm a product of a very large public school. I'm a big believer in public schools. But my son, we found out through a lot of digging, if not motivated, would be in the great middle. And the great middle in the public school system tends to be overlooked. My friends' kids who are in the top 10% of the public school system, they're going to thrive anywhere they go. Public schools are geared to the top 10% and the bottom 10 or 15%. But if you're not in either one of those, I think you can get lost. Your kid can get lost. So our son, after three years of unproductive, mediocre test scores, was not doing anything. We took him out and put him in an all boys school. The people there motivated him in such a way that he became a very good student.

Now my daughter had a learning disability and we discovered it quickly. She couldn't remember. If I taught her the

135

days of the week: Monday, Tuesday, Wednesday, in that order, I would ask a minute later what comes after Monday. She couldn't remember. She would read a sentence, see the word *home*; she saw the next sentence, she couldn't remember *home*. Short term memory disability. So she went to a special school one summer and we got a teacher there to really help her. She's now a phenomenal reader and graduated with a 3.92. And she's a killer. She got a phenomenal consulting job. She's doing great.

*   *   *

Each child is different. Some children will cry out loud, others will cry inside.

*   *   *

What's my point? My point is that, it's hard as a parent to understand your kids' needs. I think we got a little lucky and maybe were a little anal about it. I don't think it matters. I think in the end, everybody turns out okay, but I think, if I left my son in that public school, maybe it would have worked later but we would have wasted a lot of years. And my daughter needed attention, needed small classes. For different reasons, that was a good environment.

So, it's about taking the time to understand your kids and what they need and then doing something about it and not languishing.

*   *   *

Our oldest is gifted...they're all gifted, but he scores extremely high on academic tests. He also likes to be different so he has taken up music, which is certainly something I never did. He has really gravitated towards music and has no interest in, and in some cases a dislike for, sports. He started with the piano and then played the flute. Also has just picked up the bassoon because he wanted to be different. And that's not like me. He also thinks at a level that is very different. He doesn't seem to need the same sort of touch, or he gets very uncomfortable with excessive, positive reinforcement that sometimes I tend to provide. I just need to make sure that he knows that I am there for him and I'm very proud of him. I'm always asking, *Do you want to talk? You're moving into middle school, do you want to talk about that?* Sometimes I struggle to find things that he and I can do together. Our interests are a little bit different.

*   *   *

My son is smart. He is very hardworking and he's 10. I don't know if it's because he's the middle child and there is a little competitive stuff, but he is more outwardly sensitive to others. All the kids care about others, but you can see he is more outwardly sensitive. I think all of our children tend to be shy. For him, I tend to focus on how to build his confidence but make him independent at the same time. To make sure he is comfortable trying things, doing things. Sometimes he requires a lot of one on one to get through a project. I want to make sure he does it so he's confident that he can. On the other hand, the challenge is not babying him as the youngest boy and I think sometimes he likes to play that role. So I want to give him confidence but also push him to be independent.

*   *   *

What's important is to make sure they all feel close together and they're all looking out for each other. I'm always emphasizing that they're all treated the same. They try to play *Who's the favorite?* Sometimes I tell them they're all the favorite. I say, *You're all the same.* I don't know if that is good or bad, but you want to make sure that they know they have a responsibility to take care of each other.

*   *   *

When my son and I visited colleges, we described it as a road trip occasionally interrupted with a campus tour. We went to Boston and went to the basketball games and we went to three campuses. We went to Australia and we played golf together. So I just find as a man, as a father, I have to pay more attention to try to create equal opportunities for my daughters because they're not as interested in the same things as a son is. And I think that I stress over that more than they would want me to.

*   *   *

I'm maybe not as buddy buddy with my daughter, yet we schedule father/daughter time all the time. We send notes and emails to each other. We write letters to each other. We go out. She loves bookstores. I love bookstores. So we do those kinds of things. She'll come out and play catch. But my son and I are more buddy buddy.

*   *   *

Do I see a difference in how to raise a son versus how to raise a daughter? The only difference is I spend a little more time on her relative to things like physical safety and awareness. That includes dating because that's all part of the physical. Other than that, I treat her pretty much the same. But I want to make sure that she's able to take care of herself, that she doesn't do stupid things or walk into dangerous situations. The messaging is different, that's all. With my daughter, I can be subtle and she gets it right away. With my son, I may have to beat him over the head a couple of times with the same message for him to get it.

*   *   *

My daughter is obviously very different. She brought out

the softer side of my approach. My son growing up used to tell me I was different with my daughter. I told him, *That's because I'm trying to raise you to be a man. I'm not trying to raise you to be a lady. I'm hard on you because I'm raising you to be a man. I'm easy on her because I'm raising her to be a lady.* But I think females need a strong male figure in their life just as much as males do.

I think that's one of the problems that you see with some of these young girls and teen pregnancies. What they're really looking for is some male person to love them. And if you have a male person who loves you unequivocally, like your father, then you won't necessarily seek that from somewhere else. You actually learn to become more independent. And that's what I try to do with her as well. I encourage her to have her own money. Encourage her to always have it. I say, *Never go out anywhere without your own money.*

I'll never forget. This just happened maybe five or six weeks ago. I overheard her talking to her boyfriend on the phone. I wasn't eavesdropping, and I don't know what the tiff was all about, but she basically said to him, *Let me help you. Let me help you understand something. I don't need you.* That's what she said to him. *I was raised to be independent. Even when we go out, I always make sure I have my own money. I don't need you.* I'm like, *Oh my God.* He's a nice kid, don't get me wrong. He's a good kid but she was being kind of tough on him. But I think it's a reflection of her desire to be independent.

*   *   *

The two kids are very different. He's much more of a homebody. She's much more outgoing and willing to pack up and just go. She has a mind to travel. She wants to go international. So I wouldn't be surprised if she ended up working and living overseas for some length of time.

139

*   *   *

It's a good thing she's going into the law because she's got a quick wit and she's real sharp. We have a pretty good relationship. She's growing up, and all kids go through this rebellious period. So now seeing that in her is not as distressful for me as it was with my son because it's like adolescence, the sequel. I know that he went through it and came back around, and she'll go through it, too. She'll come back around, and that's part of the process.

*   *   *

Even with kids in the same family, you can't apply the same formula. Like my kids. I have two ten years apart and I couldn't apply the same formula even if they were both males or both females. I couldn't apply the same formula to both of them because they're just different. The thing that might work for one sibling won't work for the other one.

*   *   *

Never be satisfied that you've got it right; there's always more. Kids require different levels of closeness or distance. I think kids, as they go through different phases, will demand you to be slightly different. My son at 13 may have different needs versus at 15, or my daughter at 13 versus at 17 or 21. So I try to be cognizant of the kids as they are now and remember that the balance you may have thought was the balance last year may have shifted. So I agree that you want to try to strike a balance between authoritarianism and leniency, but knowing exactly where that balance is is going to be a moving target. And be open to the fact that there's probably never, ever getting it right.

*   *   *

Raising boys versus girls? That's interesting. We always had dogs when the kids were young. After we ate cereal and there was a little bit of milk left in the bottom, we put the cereal bowl down and let the dog lick it up. And I remember my daughters, when they would crawl around, they'd go up and they'd look at the cereal bowl, wonder what this was, and put it down and head out. When my son was the same age, we wouldn't have any cereal bowls left in the house. Because he'd crawl up and look at the cereal bowl, and he'd break it. He'd smash it. It was one of those things where we said to ourselves, *Hmmm, we're dealing with a different set of chromosomes here.*

*   *   *

I don't know whether consciously we've tried to raise my son differently from my daughters. But I believe his maleness brings a different point of view to the household. He and my one daughter were very similar in their athletic interests, so I was involved with their soccer and lacrosse and stuff like that. My daughters were never particularly interested in hitting a tennis ball. Any free time on the weekend, if my son sees me he goes, *Let's go play tennis.* So he will initiate -- maybe that's the word. His maleness sometimes initiates differences because of what he wants to do. He will say, *Let's go hit tennis balls,* because he wants the time with me. And maybe my daughters did that too, but they didn't express it the same way. So it's an interesting question. I'm sure we're different with him in some ways. But I don't think we bring a philosophy that says because he's got a Y chromosome, we need to do the following things differently.

*   *   *

I try to really treat them the same. I don't know whether I do or I don't. I wrestle with my daughters and I throw them up and down on the bed. I rough house with them. And I do the same thing with my son. My wife says I'm a little harder on my son, and

141

I don't know whether that's because he's a boy or he's our third. I wouldn't say physical, but I'm more direct with my son than I am with the girls. There is a little bit of a difference in the way that I handle my son versus the way I handle the girls, although from a sports perspective and just goofing off and playing and all that stuff, I try to treat them all alike.

*   *   *

My girls were easier to raise than my boys. The girls were more focused, more organized, more ambitious and more mature at the same age. The boys were dumb, and they always got caught, but they always accepted their punishment.

*   *   *

I can remember our second oldest was maybe the most intelligent if we gave everybody an IQ test. I'm pretty sure he's the most intelligent. But he was the one who disliked school the most. He was fine up through middle school but disliked high school. One of the things you've asked me here is if I would do anything different. I just would have worked hard to find a school that was more appropriate for him. He is the very anti-authority guy in his own way. He's gotten older now, he's currently back in college, he's on the Dean's List, and the president of his class. But back then if you said A, it's clearly got to be B.

*   *   *

My daughter and my wife might see this differently, but really I'd say up until around age 10, I didn't think there was too much difference in the relationship between my boys and me and my daughter and me. I really loved doing things that she did which were different from what the boys did. Her birthday parties were sometimes a craft birthday party or pajamas sleepover party. I loved being with her and her girlfriends, and I think I was as much

142

involved with those parties as I was with the boys when they did their sports thing or whatever. It was terrific. Somewhere probably around 10 or 11 years old, it became different. I could relate to the boys more naturally. With my daughter, I had to think about it. Because if I didn't think about it, it didn't happen, and then I felt at a loss. And I've had to do some things that I otherwise really wouldn't do. I'd go to the mall with my daughter, which is something I can't stand. But I had to do it just to spend time with her. I'm sensing now that's she's 21 that's starting to change a little bit. We've talked about politics and even sports.

*   *   *

I don't know where this came from but she's an Eagle's fan and a Phillies fan, so I'm thinking next summer I'll get some tickets. I'll get four tickets and take my wife, her and a friend. I've learned with my daughter, if you allow her to do it with a friend, then it goes down easier. She's into art and so I'll say, *Let's go to a museum*. I'm trying. With her it's an effort to get into her life. With the boys it was just easier to be part of theirs.

*   *   *

When your kids are young, it's highly physical but it's not as emotional. The older they get, the less the physical stuff is and the more emotional and mental. With three very different kids at very different places with very different personalities, probably the biggest challenge we faced as a parent is trying to just understand where they are and be there and support them before things get bad.

My son is big into baseball. He had a horrible situation with the coach. Just kind of marginalized. It just spiraled from there. He couldn't hit because he was so stressed. He'd walk up to the plate and no way he could hit the ball. You could tell from his body language. All season long like this. He was miserable. I told him to

143

get through it as best he could. This spring, very positive experience. Different coach, whom I'm helping as a co-coach. We won the division. He's one of the stars on the team. Same kid, different environment. For him, he's got to know he is liked, and being liked by the adult is important. His old coach just had no time for anybody. He had three kids on the team. His three kids were the rock stars and the rest of the team were supporting characters for them. It was just one of those bad situations.

He had a teacher who was a very good teacher but very disciplined, very gritty. A lot of homework. He internalized stuff to the point where he would get himself sick. Completely different than my older son. My older son would work at it, but if it didn't get done, it didn't get done. He would take life easier. It's tiring, it's a challenge, but they have to figure it all out without you. That's where I was with my parents. And all of a sudden you figure it out without them.

*   *   *

A lot of differences are in-born personality differences. I thought before we had kids that it was the environment that you create that forges their personalities. The same traits we see now are the things we saw when they were six months old. You just couldn't style a personality. They're just different people. It's difference in personality versus gender differences. My daughter from the beginning had more patience to play and focus on things for a longer period of time. She's social but in a different way. She would hang out with her friends and play. The boys rough house more and are more physical. I probably rough house more with my boys and do more sports, although I coached her softball team this year. With her, I'm cognizant of the whole father's role and self image and how important that relationship is.

But I'm not sure that I see that much gender difference. I attribute it more to personalities. I think as much as we try, probably the hardest thing is just being fully present and aware. Sometimes that's easy. When it's easy, it's great. But there are also times when I don't want to go out and play catch in the backyard, but I think they're not going to ask for that long. I keep remembering what my dad did. He'd say, *No,* so I stopped asking. And so I guess you got to take the moment where it is.

*   *   *

My takeaway is you can't preconceive what each child needs. If you try to do it your way, you're probably going to do it wrong and you're probably going to do more harm than good, even though you think you're doing good things. I hear things like, *Every child should be treated the same.* I don't believe that. I think every child has to be treated the way every child needs to be treated. We have a saying in the family: *Life isn't fair, so don't try to make everything the same as a way of getting equal treatment.* All my kids can go to college, they all can get a car, they all can get a job, they all have unlimited kinds of ability, but doing the exact same thing to every kid is probably not a good formula. You have to use multiple roles, responsibilities, techniques. Cuts pretty thick, too. Each child is different.

*   *   *

Everybody's different. That's what makes this world interesting. I can look at my kids, and there are certain things about my son that drive me nuts. He can tend to be a whiner about things. On the other hand, he's coachable in a sense that when he's angry, we let him blow off steam and then I can get to him and say, *Okay buddy. I get how you're upset about this but let's talk about it.* And he will say, *Yeah, you know what? You're right.* He's very appreciative of my insight.

My daughter, on the other hand, is a stubborn son of a gun, and it will be almost a cold day in hell before she'll say, *You know,*

145

you were right. In her mind, she is admitting that she was wrong, but my son can admit it. She is tough. And that's very tough for my wife to deal with. It's good in a way because my wife's still learning a little bit more about herself and how to deal with that situation. My daughter, I can still get through to her, usually at night because she's still - - she gets upset when I say this - - she doesn't like going upstairs without somebody going with her. The kids' bedrooms are upstairs and our bedroom is down on the first floor. She's afraid of monsters. I mean, here's a kid who's in third grade, and I'll tease her sometimes and she'll say, *Dad, don't embarrass me like that*.

When it's time to go to bed at night, she'll say the Lord's Prayer, and then she always wants a story from me. Sometimes I do it. Sometimes I'm just too tired and I'll tell her, *Honey, I'm just not ready*. But I can do a lot of teaching with her at night when it's just one-on-one with her when mom's not around. I can tell that she's soaking stuff in like a sponge.

I guess one of the things I would say is you got to look for opportunities with your kids where you can really connect with them. Maybe it's in the day time. Some people say they have some of their best conversations with their teenage kids when they're driving in the car, and your eyes are forward and they can be back there just kind of talking more candidly but not having to look directly at the parent. You got to find out what works for the kids. That's critical.

*   *   *

I probably was tougher on my sons when they were growing up. It's just easier to smack a boy when he's doing something wrong. I don't think I ever hit my daughters. My sons, on the other hand, clearly got the belt. They probably needed it more, too. Their dispositions were different. I mean, they would do stupid or more defiant things. The girls just tended to be better behaved.

146

*   *   *

My son had braces on his teeth and he was always breaking the brackets. He wasn't just breaking rubber bands like everybody does. He was breaking the brackets and he would have to go back to the dentist. That's one thing that didn't cost us anything really. He went through three or four of those TI calculators that they had to have in high school. The first one was stolen. Okay, we cut him slack. We bought him the second one. The second one got stolen. I said, *You're buying the third one.* And he had to buy the glasses that he broke, so we hit him in the pocketbook early on. We said, *You're being irresponsible and you're just showing that you don't care, so if you want another pair, you're going to pay for them.* He had an iPod stolen from a party at the shore last summer. He replaced his iPod and it got stolen again when he was teaching. He basically put it on the kids and said, *I want the iPod back. I'm not going to punish anyone as long as it gets back to me, but otherwise I'm going to track down who did it.* It got back to him but he lost all of his music. But he learned some responsibility and I think that's the only way to do it.

*   *   *

This summer, my son's job is delivering wings on his bike. No, on his sister's bike. He didn't have his own. Classic example. He's living with four guys in this house and they were all over at our house one day. My wife, knowing exactly what she's doing, asks Harry, *What are you doing, Harry? Mrs. Jones, I'm in law school. I got one more year. Oh, so in May you're going to graduate from law school. You're going to be a lawyer!* She looks at my son. And then she asks another kid, *Kevin, what are you doing? I'm in veterinary school. Oh, so when you graduate you're going to be a doctor!* She goes for the third kid. *Joe, what are you doing?* He said, *Mrs. Jones, I'm not really doing anything, but you know, when your son can't make it, I substitute for him delivering wings.* She's said it just blew up in her face. I guess I should feel better than Mrs. Kawolski: at least my kid's the regular wing man and hers is the substitute. I was like, *God help us*.

But he did say to us late in the summer, *I'm getting tired of being the guy who doesn't have any money. I'm tired of being the guy who doesn't have his act together.* Now that he's teaching full-time, he's getting a feel for it. He's coming around but still doesn't have any cash, which is why I think I have to have a budget conversation with him because my wife has the feeling that some of the money might be going into smoking substances. I'm not sure what else could be why he doesn't have any cash. His expenses are not that high, and he's always made no qualms about the fact that smoking pot is no big deal. I hope and pray and believe that he would never do anything much more serious than that, but you never know.

*   *   *

That's another one where my wife is black and white. The two older ones are going to church every single week. The two younger ones are pretty much like, *Yeah right*. My one daughter actually is thinking about examining all world religions. She says, *Who says the Catholics have it right?* She dated a guy for a while who was one of these, *There's no God. There's just kind of like a universal life force and we're all a part of the universal life force.* I'm like, *I'm going to extinguish your universal life force, you ass.* I think the Jesuits encourage that. And my daughter hasn't been going to church with us at all. When we're together somewhere as a family, she'll go sometimes just to make us happy, but she's clearly not looking at herself as being Catholic right now. My son is mostly lazy and he's even said things like, *I'm sure I'll raise my kids Catholic when I get married.* But it's just not convenient for him to have to go to church and to deal with that kind of stuff. Again, it's just amazing to me. My kids, there's less than five years from the oldest to the youngest, and yet with the two older ones, it's almost like they're from a different family.

148

*   *   *

The goal should be to get to know each kid as a person, not just as your child.

*   *   *

I thought my son would never go to college and make a living. It turns out, he applied to six schools and got into all of them. He tells friends he went to Rutgers University on a fall afternoon, went to a party and got drunk, and got sober in the spring. I don't know if he ever went to class or not. I don't remember his exact grade point, but he failed and I just pulled him out. We tried to send him to community college, but they wouldn't have him. I told him, *You just go to work. You're on your own.* He fooled around with dead end jobs for a couple of years. Then he found his passion for working with kids. He became a teacher's assistant in school. This school handled difficult children. A private school where public schools would send their kids who they couldn't handle but for whom they had to legally provide an education. He loves it but can't get a job as a teacher because he had to have a college degree. Now he gets a chance. He goes back to school. He's now involved in social work. He's got one more semester to go and he'll graduate in the spring. He's on the Dean's list. He's got a 3.75 average, president of his class. But it's because of maturity, number one. And number two, he found a passion and he knew what he needed to do. So okay. He'll do what he has to do to get what he wants to get.

*   *   *

I have a son who is 27 years old. I have a daughter who's 24. I would say that I have an unusually good relationship with both of them. Although these days in some ways I'm closer with my son than I am with my daughter, and that's her choosing. Growing up I was probably a little bit closer to my daughter than

149

my son. When she was a kid, even through most of high school, she'd throw herself in my lap. As she's become more of an adult, she's become a bit more distant. And I think part of that is she's probably a little self absorbed. My son and I, we talk almost every day. There's almost no advice. He doesn't call me for advice or help. It's always very casual. He's my buddy, and I might even say that he's the person who I'm closest to in this world. He knows me well. We have some common interests and we're involved in each other's lives. He's very open about what's going on with him, good and bad. If he's having a problem with a girl, he'll tell me about it. When he becomes intimate with a girl, he'll tell me. It's not that I'm probing. It's his nature. He'll talk about it. My daughter tends to be more careful with her personal information.

*   *   *

My son. People really like him. He's a very nice guy. He's sensitive. He's a very good listener. He would be the kid that calls me up on the phone and says, *How you doing? How was that thing yesterday? How'd you golf today?* He really cares. He's a very caring guy. Women like him because he has tremendous respect for women. My son's a very, very nice person. I mean fundamentally to the core. He's smart. I wouldn't call him a guy with super confidence in every part of his life. He's a normal guy but won't take shit from anybody. Deals with confrontation, by the way, beautifully. Way better than I ever did. He's really meant to be a litigator I think. You can't rattle my son. When we have arguments today, I'm frequently the person, shades of my father, who gets worked up. And he'll say, *I think you ought to calm yourself down. Maybe it's a good time for you to calm yourself down and let's discuss this.* He's that kind of a guy; very cool headed. If you met him, you'd really like him. Travels the country; travels the world. My kids have both have traveled way more than I have. My daughter in particular. She was arrested for drinking at a house in Berwyn, but she was a total goodie two shoes. I picked her up and gave her a hug. She was so upset by it and beat herself up. I didn't see any reason to ground her. Ground her? What for? It wasn't anything so bad. She had a beer. And when the cops came the really drunk kids all jumped out the windows of the first floor. She was in the basement.

*   *   *

Girls are tough because they hold grudges. Guys, you kick them in the ass and that's it. Whereas girls, mothers and daughters... I see my wife and her mother, how their grudges can be held for a long time.

*   *   *

Raising boys versus girls. Is it the same? Is it different? I think that girls are about between 8 and 60 times harder. My total experience equals one boy and one girl, but if you ask me to generalize based on one and one, girls are way harder. They have a long memory. With my son, when we have a fight or a disagreement over something, it ends in three minutes and we're on to the next topic. My daughter clearly holds onto things that she perceives to be a violation. There's a thousand examples. My family doesn't get together very often, but a couple of years ago we went to restaurant in Philadelphia as a foursome, which is sort of cool. So I'm the driver and we get to the restaurant and I find a spot on Market Street. It's amazing. I'm very excited. Parallel park into the parking spot. My wife is next to me. My daughter is behind me. My son is diagonally behind me. I stopped the car and I said to my daughter, *Jennifer, make sure you're careful before you open the door.* She doesn't say anything to me. Because she didn't say anything to me, I felt the need when she cracked the door to say, *Hey. There's a car coming!* She got out of the car and she stopped talking to me. She was insulted that I didn't trust her. She wouldn't look at me for the entire meal. Didn't want anything to do with me.

151

We get three quarters through the meal and I said, *Listen. I'm sure you're mad at me. I'm sure that I was even an asshole. I accept all that but don't I have enough good will built up that you can let me off on this one? Can't you find a way to let me off on this very serious offense which was insulting you by saying twice something that you apparently already knew?* Breaking through to her was very hard. With my son, it never would have gone like that. Never. So I will confess to you that, and there's really nothing to be proud of, she scares me a little bit. My daughter.

With my son, it's like everything's on the table. You're mad, you're happy, you're sad. Whatever it is, it's right in front of us. We'll deal with it. My daughter? I always think that the wheels are always turning. So I think girls are way harder than boys.

*   *   *

I think daughters are way more complicated. I certainly can't generalize and speak for fathers and daughters at large, but that's my experience and in some cases my observation of other dads and daughters, or just daughters by themselves. My daughter certainly spoke less about the things that were bothering her. She kept things inside of her and my son didn't. He never kept things inside. So I always thought that made it harder for me as a parent. I think she's less forgiving for my failures and my faults than my son is. It seems like he has the maturity to say, *This dad of mine, he's a pretty good guy. He did okay, but he's clearly an imperfect being.* My daughter probably secretly says I sort of came up short in these three areas. I think she's keeping score.

*   *   *

The biggest challenge as a father is trying to relate to three totally different individuals. It's not being a father to a son. It's being a father to son three fold because each one of them is so different. Maybe going out and roughhousing with one while

152

another would rather sit and play Pokémon. I want to spend more one on one time with them. Pull each away from the other two. It's such a pleasant event when you do that. It really is. It's just, there's no noise outside of the interaction when it's one on one. We have three and we have friends who have six, and we have friends who have one. The couple with one will tell you it's the hardest thing in the world and the couple with six will say, *After three, it's like you can have eleven.*

*　　*　　*

As a father, I needed to adjust my style for each of my two boys. They were different. One was short and shy. The other was tall and outgoing. One was focused, very caring and listened well. The other had ADD and got easily bored. One studied hard and had to work to get good grades. The other did well in school without working, and if I pushed him, he would push away. Now they are adults. I am close to both of them. They both come to me for advice. One works with me and we're together daily. It's my biggest joy in life. I am so proud of him and with how motivated he is to help his clients. I talk to the other probably twice a day.

*　　*　　*

All kids are different. Don't try to clone them. If you do, you will develop an average that may be intimidating to some and hold back others. Plant seeds but don't dictate. The challenge is to learn how <u>you</u> need to adapt to each kid.

*　　*　　*

My kids are 10 years apart so I was a very different parent with my son versus with my daughter. I think part of that was because of external factors that I didn't have any control over. When my son was younger, I was working full-time and going to school full-time at night. We had no money and we had this old

153

beat up old car that sometimes would start and sometimes wouldn't. My job was to get him to school in the morning. This car would die and sometimes I would end up standing out thumbing a ride to take him up to daycare. Then I would take the bus and come back downtown. We were going through all of those struggles and trying to build a life. So I didn't really see that much of him. I was just doing what I felt I had to do in order to make ends meet. Now what's interesting is you fast forward ten years later and he's 10 years old, my daughter is born and at that point, I'm at a different stage. I made a conscious decision to try to be more involved in my daughter's life in the early stages. With my son, I missed everything. I missed the walking and the talking. I missed everything. I didn't want to repeat that mistake with her.

*　　　*　　　*

Each of my kids is different. I see confidence and lack of confidence. Strong motivation and lack of motivation. I was stricter with the older one - - probably too strict.

*　　　*　　　*

I have two daughters. They ask me once in a while, *Are you ever disappointed you never had a son? Did you want a son instead of a daughter?* I tell them that all my life I was never disappointed that they were girls. Never once. I think I tried to treat them the same regardless of if they were boys or girls. But I noticed I was getting really angry with my 15 year old last week who was mouthing off. And I said to myself if she was a son, I think I'd probably punch her right in the frickin head. So maybe that is a difference in terms of philosophy. Things could possibly play out from a disciplinary standpoint a little bit differently. Otherwise I think I treat them in the same way I'd treat sons.

*　　　*　　　*

Kids...Different Kids

Questions:

1 *Are your kids different from each other? How? Are they the same in other ways? How so?*

2 *A lot of these fathers stressed the need to get to know each kid as an individual and to be prepared to treat them differently? Do you agree?*

3 *A lot of them also said it was important to spend time with each of them individually. Do you agree?*

4 *If these suggestions make sense to you, how well are you doing? Do you need to do something different?*

Discipline

I want to be heard, so I talk less.

We all want to be liked by our kids. But we also need to be disciplinarians, to make tough calls. You need to set boundaries and rules.

So identify what behaviors in your kids would make you the most proud. And then, everyday, simply do the things that promote that behavior.

Stick to your guns.

I think what you want, what you're trying to do in this crazy world, is to give them the judgment to make decisions.

The kids were basically good kids. Did they do pot or anything like that? They probably did. One of their friends did a video. My daughter's showing it to us one night and my wife says, *That's our house!* There were pictures of beer and stuff like that but we didn't know about it.

156

*   *   *

I was wild as a kid. I stole cars and we'd try anything. I don't want to be totally hypocritical.

*   *   *

Whatever rules we had were to protect them, to make sure they didn't get hurt. The last thing you want is to see your kids get hurt. Particularly when they start dating. I suffered a lot of hurt as a kid, and I didn't want my kids to have that type of pain.

*   *   *

I really learned a lot from my wife. I would have been a lot more physical with them than I ended up being. I would have thought nothing of just smacking them on the rump or bopping them on the head or something like that. But my wife was absolutely adamant that is not what you do with children, and it didn't take me long to fall in line. And so basically we raised our kids and never spanked them. We just didn't do it. And in retrospect, that worked. I'm sure there was an occasional swat on the bottom when they were in harm's way or if we had to drive a point home that was particularly important. But on balance, there was no such thing as a whipping. We just didn't have those. And almost never did I do things out of anger. I don't ever recall being so angry at my kids, even when they did something I didn't want them to do, that it would result in a spanking. We disciplined for effect and not as a relief of our own frustrations.

*   *   *

We both wanted the best for them. We both understood that Rome was neither built nor destroyed in a day. So whatever decision we were making was not likely to have such weighty consequences that it mattered a great deal. When things did

157

matter? I remember one time my wife said to me that when my son starting driving, she told him he needed to stop at the stop sign. He couldn't just come to a rolling stop and squeak through. And he gave her some snappy comment like, *I see it.* And she came home and asked me how I felt about it, and if I felt a certain way, would I say something to him? One difference between us is I don't mind confrontation and she does. So if there was a confrontation to be had, then I damn sure wouldn't duck it. I just got both of them together and I said, *Here's what I understand your mom said and here's what I understand your response was. And the only thing I can tell you is that if you don't do it our way, you're not going to drive.* And he is a terrific driver.

*   *   *

When you're kids start to drive, you're in a totally different situation. You don't go to sleep until hearing that car come in.

*   *   *

We had confrontations, and I won some of them and I lost some of them. I have absolutely no advice except this. One, God forbid something should happen. You have at least done your best to send the child in a different direction. Number two, there should never be any doubt in your kid's mind about how you feel. The first one is if anything should happen, at least you've done your best to steer the ship in a different direction. The second thing is that if anything happens, and they survive it, maybe they can use that as a kind of talking point for themselves and say, *That's what dad meant.*

*   *   *

A big challenge is not to worry about making a mistake. Sure, you will make mistakes but I think you will remember them longer than your kids will.

158

*　　*　　*

It is a journey. The last thing you want to do is to damage your relationship to the point to where the journey gets to be impossible. It's very important that you say things in a way that people can hear them. Because if they can't hear you, it doesn't make any difference. But the mistake I make, and I think a lot of people make, is if I have a point of view, I need to learn to say it in a way that's acceptable to you. I can't call you an asshole. I can't embarrass you in public and think for one minute that you're going to hear what I have to say because I have so offended what it is that you stand for. It's the same with kids.

Ben Franklin was a genius at this. He always said things in a way that other people could hear. So if he disagreed, he talked about his inability to understand the total point. If he wanted you to turn left, he'd let you know that he was perfectly willing to turn right if that's the direction we needed to go in. And so when you ended up with the conversation with Franklin, you always found yourself listening because he said things so you could hear them; not so he could beat his chest or flap his jaws.

That's what I'm saying. It's not kindness. Stop and think. The difference between yelling at a kid and telling him that you're going to kick his ass if you catch him on a motorcycle. The difference between that and saying, *I'm giving you my point of view and I would appreciate your conforming to that.* It's not a journey you can travel beyond that. What are you going to do? Sue them? Every now and then I get myself in a situation in which I promise to do something I'm not going to do. Somebody calls your bluff, and you're in trouble.

*　　*　　*

I want to be heard, so I talk less.

*   *   *

I live in classic suburban white America. I'm not a classic suburban white guy. My background is different. Again, my approach to disciplining is very different from much of what I see in the suburbs. I don't suffer fools gladly. And my kids see that. I just think that they see a big difference. For example, I don't know how many of their friends weren't allowed to do instant messaging until they were in high school. You can make the arguments whether it's good or bad, but it's just certain things that I believe in that I don't compromise.

*   *   *

How do I discipline my kids? Well, I try to show them the right way to do things by my own behavior. By talking to them and probably a little too often, if I have to, by yelling at them. And by the traditional ways of discipline, like timeouts and taking away privileges.

*   *   *

I want to be a good father. Not a friend. I've always kind of gotten ticked off with the people who say they want to be friends with their kids. You don't want to be their enemy, obviously, and you don't just want to be viewed as strictly an authoritarian. I've always thought you should be as close as you can with your kids. You certainly can do things that they enjoy and play with them and take them places and have a lot of fun with them. But you're not their buddy, and if you become more of their buddy than their parent, almost inevitably there's going to be some kind of a break. You can't be a disciplinarian and be their best friend. It's tough one minute to be correcting them and in the next, saying, *Let's go fishing*. It just doesn't work. At least not for me.

*   *   *

160

Different strokes I suppose. I mean I want the same things for my kids. I want them to be confident. I want them to be independent, and I want them to be successful. I want them to be happy, but I'm not so sure that having no rules and no boundaries is a way to achieve that.

*　　*　　*

I don't think I'm an unhappy guy. I don't think I lack confidence. I respected and listened to my dad. I enjoyed spending time with him. But he had set strict rules and strict boundaries, and it was clear there would be repercussions if I violated them. And I do that same thing with my kids. I think my kids respect me. At least right now they enjoy spending time with me. Whether they will as teenagers or not, I don't know. But I wouldn't be able to do that if I let them run free, run wild. I've seen kids who act that way, and their parents don't do much about it. My brother and sister-in-law. Their kid, he is a pistol that kid. And they let him pretty much do whatever he wants. The kid's five years old and it's Christmas at my in-laws' house. We're sitting around having a nice conversation. All of a sudden he stands up and yells, *This party sucks, and all of you people suck!*

*　　*　　*

Somebody gave me a book called "Difficult Conversations." Have you seen it? It was in the business context of how important it is to have difficult conversations. And I always found in the business context, I actually enjoy them. I get sort of geared up for talking to an employee, say, about being an alcoholic and having to leave the company. You know, I didn't revel in that, didn't enjoy it, but I kind of enjoyed the challenge. So having difficult conversations is key, including with your kids.

*　　*　　*

When our kids were growing up, we found ourselves having different groups of friends than we had in the past. We no longer hung out with some people who used to be our friends. We hung out with people whose kids were like what we wanted ours to be like. One of my friends' kids would come over my house and my wife said we've got to remove everything from the table because one kid's a maniac. Guess what? I didn't invite them over any more. I started seeing in other people's kids the way I wanted my kids to be. And we hung out with them as opposed to some others.

*　　　*　　　*

How do you want your kids to be when they're little kids and you're going to somebody's house? At my mother's house, there's stuff on the tables. When my brother's kids came to mother's house, she had to remove all the knick knacks because the kids were going to grab them and throw them and knock stuff over. My kids came and didn't touch them.

*　　　*　　　*

Discipline was more of an issue with my son. For example, to start off with, whether he had ADHD or not, I'd say, *If you're not doing well in school, or if you're bringing home bad grades, or you're not telling me about bad grades, guess what, you start losing privileges. No videogames. No play time.* All the way up to no visits with friends. I mean, you start taking away luxuries. I do that.

We went through all that with him, but it didn't work. So we tried the carrot, and that really didn't work. So we tried something else. In the summer before he started high school, we sent him on a two week, pretty rugged outward bound excursion, alone. No friends. He just met a group in Utah and spent two weeks roughing it in the back country. Canoeing and rafting. We told him why we were sending him.

He needed to learn some self respect. I told him, *You got to learn how to take care of yourself. You need to learn to take some responsibility. And you can't use having ADHD as an excuse for everything. Understand that there are certain things that you're going to find harder, but it's not an excuse to not achieve. You have to find a way to work with your issues and still succeed and you've got to do it on your own.*

So we sent him away for two weeks, and I think it had a profound effect. Absolutely profound. More than I would have hoped for. And when we picked him up at the airport after two weeks. It was 2:00 in the morning when the flight finally got in. You saw it in his eyes. He got off that plane and he was almost in tears because he was so happy to be home. He came home with an absolute new appreciation for what he had. Absolutely. And really from that day, we've seen a marked difference in how he responds to us. So that was good. That was really good. It's not perfect, but it did make a huge difference.

*   *   *

I totally forbade them for a long time to do instant messaging. I forbade them from having text messaging. I said, *You're not allowed.* Now just relatively recently, I relaxed it. I said, *You're older now.* I would not let them do it when I didn't feel they could be responsible enough. So my daughter is now 13 and she is actually now, for the first time, allowed to text. She's very responsible so I don't really worry, but the deal we have with them on their emails, on their Facebooks and all that stuff, now that we're letting them do social media, is that mom and dad have the right any time to review everything without asking their permission. *So if you're going to do this, fine. You are not allowed to have secrets and that's the way it is. If you don't like it, I can just turn everything off.* I really didn't give them an option.

163

But since I was so strict when they were growing up, it's been easier for me. They know it doesn't do any good to say, *So and so's parents...* They know that will just piss me off because I don't care what other people do. I never did. They know that. They don't even bring it up. They just accept that's the way it is, and it's interesting. I believe they understand that mom would be even stricter than dad. And matter of fact, mom did not want to give them email. Dad's the one who said, *Look, they're old enough now.*

*   *   *

Decide what you think "good" looks like. You get that by experiencing a whole range of other people's kids and deciding which ones you'd rather yours be like. Which ones you'd be more proud of. So identify what behaviors in your kids would make you the most proud. And then, everyday, simply, do the things that promote that behavior.

*   *   *

My kids would tell you they can never remember a time that we had to spank them or anything like that. I'm sure we did a couple times when they were very young but never had to do it again. There was no confusion that I was the boss. No confusion. No talk back to dad. Now I don't want to act like it was militaristic, but there was no confusion about who was in charge. And there was also no confusion about who their biggest fan was. Ever. Going to every soccer game or every sporting event, being visible, being there. Never any confusion in my kids' minds about who their biggest fan was.

*   *   *

I have a friend right now whose son keeps getting speeding tickets and caught for underage drinking. He had to go to Camden

164

last week to get his son because this kid's 16, at a concert, and he was drunk and wandering around Camden. Somebody called him. I wouldn't have told anybody any of the stories about my son that this guy was telling me, with some pride, about what a screw off his kid is. Like, *Wait till you hear what Charlie did this week.* You'd have to put bamboo shoots under my nails to tell a story like that. Another friend of mine is proud about the after party at the junior prom. How all of his daughter's friends were all trashed. You know, the things some people are proud of, I would be embarrassed by. I don't know where they get their definition of what success looks like as far as raising their kids goes.

*   *   *

I'm more of the disciplinarian. I look at discipline as consistency and building boundaries. I think there is a role that usually falls to the father but it can be combined or it could be the mother. The role of those boundaries is to protect. So understanding rules, understanding society's rules, understanding what other people need and being able to relate to other people politely, those things are important for me. My daughter likes to push against the rules. I actually give her kudos for pushing against them. I listen and I encourage her to test the limits. But there's knowing what's right and letting your kids know what's right. I'm a bit worried about my son. There's a joke that I'm saving for my daughter's education and my son's bail money. He's a really great kid, but I think he's too easily influenced by his friends. My daughter is very grounded. We'll see how things end up playing out.

*   *   *

Can I say *No* to my kids? Some parents seem unable to. I feel like I know when to say *No* and how to say it. I don't believe in giving kids everything. We need to teach responsibility.

165

*　　*　　*

Teach kids that it's okay to lose. These days, they play baseball and they don't want to keep score. One of the greatest lessons in life, I believe, is when you lose, how do you lose? How are you and who are you when you lose? If you get that one down, that's pretty cool.

*　　*　　*

My brother throws his 19 year old daughter out of the house every other week. Sometimes she stays at her boyfriend's. He withdraws his love. He's emotionally abusive. That's something very deadly. Your first principle is to keep her safe. I'm sure you can get to the point where you're completely sheltering her, but that's not what you want. I would say to my daughter, *I really love you. This is why I need to do this. It may be a little embarrassing, and you don't want me to do this. But know that I love you, and thus I'm compelled to do this. I think it's the right thing for me to do as a father.* But then, everybody's different. It's so tricky being a father.

*　　*　　*

Kids need boundaries. We all need boundaries actually. Adults need boundaries too. Kids need to learn boundaries, and it is almost always the father that takes that role. And without that role, they struggle. They can struggle tremendously in not knowing what their limits are and not understanding what other people's limits are. Even when they're pushing against it, they have to have a boundary. But in our culture, we've gotten to a point where people are afraid to offend their kids. So we're raising kids without boundaries. It's not healthy. Psychologically, you know that it's not healthy. Sometimes love is right to say, *No.* It's creating boundaries. It's the way you do it. To me, it's all in the way you do it. Do you love your kids or do you withdraw love because they

166

violated the boundaries? They're going to violate the boundaries sometimes. But you still love them and still try to teach them.

*   *   *

It's a tough balancing act, isn't it? I mean, my daughter went away for school, and we literally talked on the phone every day most of freshman year. She's telling me a lot of things. She failed a final in her first semester. She was up late studying. She got a call from her roommate who was drunk, and my daughter dropped everything and went to pick up her roommate. And I said to her, *You did the right thing.* I always told her I didn't want her going out drinking and doing drugs, but if ever she's out and she has been drinking, not to drive. I said, *If the person you're with is drinking, don't get into the car with them. Take a taxi home. I'll pay for it. I'll come and get you. No questions asked.* She never drank. If she did, she certainly didn't drink much. She hardly drinks now. So I said, *You did the right thing. That was the right thing. People are more important. You can make up the class.*

Two months later, she comes home for spring break, and she didn't want to go back to school. It was a tough conversation: *You got to go back. You can't make me go back. You're right, I can't make you. I can't physically make you but you have to go back. You have to trust me that you'll get through this freshman year stuff. No, I don't want to go back.* Part of it was her boyfriend was at another school. And ultimately we got into a yelling match. We both pulled back. The next morning she was supposed to be in class. She didn't go right away and I said, *You're going. You have to go. There are no ifs, ands, or buts, you have to go. We'll talk all about it later but you have to go.*

Thankfully, she went. But man, I was so scared that I was going to lose her right at that point. And having gone from literally talking every day to where we're about to split. Like, how do you know what was right? I don't know that that was right even now,

167

although she went, and finished. Did fine in school and all that. I would say I failed in that moment in the sense that I was clueless as to what was right. I yelled. In the end it seemed to work out. It was a tough time.

*   *   *

Nothing magic here: discipline is hard. You can't be wishy-washy but you don't want to overreact either. Dads can be more irrational than their kids, but you need to act when it's required.

*   *   *

Much easier to loosen things up than it is to tighten it back down. You're going to get a lot of resistance. They're going to view it as taking freedoms away. Taking their God-given rights away from them. So for me, you start strict. I think they need strict when they're young. But it's not just strict because these are the rules. It's strict with an explanation of why. They don't have to agree with my rationale but they deserve to understand the rationale. Always. I never believed in just giving them rules and saying, *That's the way it is because I'm your father.* I'll say, *This is the way it is. This is the reason why.* If you don't take the time to make sure that they understand your rationale, then they don't learn. They don't have to agree, but they'll at least learn that it's not just a whim.

So if you say, *I don't want you to do this now because you're too young and I don't believe it's safe*, they innately know that you're giving them respect by explaining. When you don't explain to them, I believe they take that as a sign of disrespect. They don't verbalize it. They may not even consciously think it. Even when I'm mad at them, I don't do it disrespectfully. Even if I fly off the handle, it's human, I will apologize. It's not blind discipline. You got to treat them like people. You got to treat them the way you would want to be treated. So whenever we said *No* to

168

anything, we told them why.

And then when we eased up and allowed them some additional privileges, we would explain to them why and then what's expected of them in return. *Alright, I'm going to let you have this luxury, but here's what you have to do in return. Here are the conditions. And if you break the rules, there is a consequence.* Those are important things.

*   *   *

I was a hard ass with him, no doubt. But I looked at where a lot of his contemporaries were going and the kinds of things that they were doing. Like kids with the pants dragging below their waist. I just didn't tolerate that and he knew it. I said, *You can do what you want to do. But if I ever see you walking down the street with your pants dragging around your butt like that, I'm going to jump out of the car while the car is still moving and beat you to a pulp.* He knew that I wasn't playing. He knew I was serious. That's all he needed to know.

*   *   *

My oldest one was much more the Steady Eddie. We had some problems with underage drinking but never huge problems other than that. He went to college and my wife and I couldn't believe how dirty his apartment was. We were pretty sure that just judging by the empty beer bottles around that he was drinking too much. But he matriculated in four years. He became an accountant.

*   *   *

Well, my style was to get control of the kids early on. And I mean like 2 or 3 years old. You wait until your child is 7, 8, 9, 10 years old to start disciplining them, and even things like taking them out to dinner, showing which fork to use and how to sit,

169

become problems. If you start too late, then I think that's when you have to do a lot of things you don't want to have to do when their older. I mean it's in the Bible. You bend a twig while it's young so you don't have to break it when it gets old. And my wife and I were in lock step on that. Now I say we were in lock step but her perspective was, *Oh you're being too hard on them.* And I would say to her, *That's fine.* That's why you have two parents. One to be hard and one to be soft. It takes both. You can't both be hard or both be soft. You need the balance.

*   *   *

My wife and I talked about things like not wanting to raise the child to be violent or to engage in violent activities. I like to tell this story. We were just trying to be good parents. We were young. 22 years old when he was born. And we said that we weren't going to buy any violent toys like guns or things of that sort. We didn't want to raise him that way. We didn't want him handling guns.

So I remember one day coming home from work a little early and I stopped by the daycare center where he was playing outside. Rather than just walk up like I normally did, I just kind of hung back to watch the kids at play. I looked over and he and one of the other kids were playing. The one kid had a toy gun in his hand, and he was *Bam.* My son didn't have a gun but he was using his finger. They were playing *Shootem up.* So I went over and got a little closer, and he finally saw me. And he says, *Hey daddy, how you doing?* I said, *I'm fine. What is that in your hand?* He showed me he had a trigger in his hand. Just a trigger. So I said, *What's that?"* And he said, *That's a trigger because we wanted play Cowboys and Indians, and I told my friend that you didn't let me play with guns so he broke the trigger off of his gun and gave me the trigger and he kept the gun.* The kid's 3 years old. *You said I couldn't play with guns. You didn't say I couldn't play with the trigger.*

*   *   *

So the point is that you can't legislate behavior with the kids any more than you can legislate behavior in society in general. Right? I mean if you raise the kid the right way, he's not going to turn into an axe murderer. So a child can be raised in a room full of guns, but if you raise them the right way that's not going to be a problem. A lot of people would disagree with me. The environment and peer pressure and all the rest. People who are out there shooting folks are the ones who see their parents shooting folks. That's where that comes from. It's not the people who are taking their kids to the range or taking them out hunting. Or even just having weapons in the home. That's not a problem, if you teach your children to respect other people, and respect other people's property and respect human life.

*   *   *

My mother was tough. Yeah, she was pretty tough. She instilled going to church and getting an education. And the other thing she instilled very early on was that if you got in trouble and went to jail, then don't call her because she's not coming to get you.

*   *   *

My son is like a hyper clone of myself and it actually scared me a couple of months ago when I was talking to him. He's 27 years old and last year he made $225K. He's selling software to the federal government for this company in D.C. He is a workaholic maniac and is everything he had said that I was that he didn't want to be.

Actually, he's thanked me for kicking his butt when he was young. He told me, *I wouldn't be where I am today if you hadn't done that.* He told me when we were at his bachelor party that he

171

never did drugs or anything like that. He admitted to sneaking beer when he was younger, but kids always do that sort of thing. He was always mindful of what I taught him. He knew people who were doing drugs. He was around it but he never took part in it.

I think he had a certain amount of fear of me. I think that was deliberate on my part because he's bigger than I am. And I knew very early on that I was going to have to put the fear of God in him because he could probably beat me, but he didn't know that he could beat me.

*　　*　　*

My son and I, we locked horns. But he came back and told me that he appreciated it now. But he didn't really understand then what I was trying to do. So I just say, stick to your guns.

*　　*　　*

I was a bit of a difficult kid. I had periods of not doing well at college mostly because I was just having fun and not applying myself. That disappointed my dad, and we would fight nonstop. Then it all turned. He made a great decision. I was in a school that he was paying for, and I came home with bad grades for the third semester in a row. Just barely enough to get by and not get kicked out. He said, *I'm not paying anymore. If you want to go back this fall, you're going to pay your own way.* I was his oldest, and he was putting at risk whether or not I'm going to go to college. But he did it. I worked for a year or so because I had to earn enough money. They were shit jobs which I hated, which was the biggest learning experience. Learning that I didn't want to do shit jobs.

And so I went back when I had enough money, but I had to live at home. I just had enough money to pay tuition. I got a 4.0 in my first semester and I'll never forget my dad's reaction when coming home from school. I was whining about the noise at the

172

library being too loud to study. He said, *You asshole. When I paid for your school you never <u>saw</u> the library. Or you were the one making the racket in there.* Of course he was very proud at that point because he had made the right decision.

I flew through school. My father actually wound up helping me with tuition because I got a job that was more like an unpaid internship that was in my field. From that point on, we were pretty much best friends.

*   *   *

My daughters had boyfriends, some of whom I couldn't stand to look at. We always insisted on meeting every boy before they went out. I remember what a shock it was when my daughter said we didn't need to drive - - the boy would drive.

*   *   *

I am willing to discuss anything with them. But I will deny I ever drank and drove or ever tried drugs. I will deny it to the grave. This helps enforce the zero tolerance policy. Aside from that, I can't think of a topic I won't talk about. We tried to teach the kids that it's OK to disagree, but you have to respect other opinions. But there are things like religion, sex and politics that should stay in the house.

*   *   *

You know, we get in fights. We yell at them. We never spanked them or anything but we'll get in their face especially when someone's bad. I remember with Emma, who's been nicknamed at an early age by my wife, Emma Bin Laden. I remember being in a new town and we were driving around, just looking at things, and Emma didn't want to be in the car and was needling everyone. And I finally snapped. I pulled over. I said, *Get*

173

out of the car, and I drove away. She was 8. We just went around the corner and when we came back, she's there with her arms crossed. I say, *Get back in the car*. She says, *No*.

Another time we brought her to the Portland juvenile prison and dragged her through the front door and said, *I'm leaving you here*. So we're pretty strict with them when they're misbehaving. We were driving them to camp and the two of them were fighting and I was just pissed. And they say to me, *We're supposed to fight. We're brother and sister. Lighten up*. And they were right. Of course we fought like cats and dogs with our siblings.

* * *

Our kids were great from the time they were very little. I mean even at 2 and 3, very well mannered, not difficult to discipline. We didn't need to have timeouts or anything to get them under control. They were always pretty much self-controlled and I attribute that mostly to our view to raise our children so they can be part of a family. The best compliment anybody could ever give me is that it's great to be around my kids. It's a reflection of what you've done as a parent when people enjoy your children.

* * *

We never really had to discipline. Discipline for our kids was if we were disappointed in what they did, they got the message. We didn't need a lot of sanctions or penalties. My discipline was setting high expectations. They knew when they had done something wrong. This disappointment was enough to discipline them. It didn't require anything else.

* * *

They all had cars and I said, *If you ever violate the no drinking rule, you've broken one of the sacrosanct rules. The corollary to having made that rule is that if you ever need anything, you only have to make a phone call and I will be there.*

* * *

People are welcome in our house. When my kids were going through high school, to the extent they were drinking, which we didn't truly endorse but you couldn't ignore, a couple times when it happened at our house, simple rule: *You pull up. I take all your keys. They're under my pillow. You're not leaving my house. If you're drinking at my house, you're not leaving my house.* We had some sleepovers with 15 and 17 year old girls who are all drinking beer but they were safe within the house. When there were graduation parties, God help the poor kid who came thinking he was going to drink before, stop by and leave. I'd beat the shit out of him. I'd take the car, or block it in, or take the air out of the tires. If they didn't give me their keys, they weren't allowed in the house. So we've always felt that it was important that they get the whole concept of a safe environment, which becomes a nurturing environment, which becomes a good environment for self development and confidence.

* * *

One of the things that I found with my kids is they can be totally annoyed about something, I mean really pissed, and I can say to them, *You know what, I get it. When I was your age, I felt the same way.* I acknowledge what they're feeling, but then I also try to teach and tell them why what they did wasn't the best choice. I think that that makes it much more believable. I don't think people, and particularly kids, respond well to just being commanded and dictated to. I think you can still get to the same result without being that way, and it can be a much more effective way of getting across your points. It's very easy to point out the negative things in what your kids are doing and gloss over the positive things because that's what's expected. People respond so

175

much better to encouragement than they do negative stuff. And that's not to say that I don't point out bad choices that my kids make, but again, it's the way you do it, because at the end of the day, I think you want to try to build people up rather than tear them down. My view is that kids are going to respond much better to a generally positive way of dealing with them.

*   *   *

My mother tended to be a real stickler and she was tough. She was a taskmaster, in part because my father was working a lot just to make ends meet. So he wasn't around that much. My mother's personality was such that if there was a problem, she wasn't going to say, *Wait until your father comes home*. She was dealing with it then. That was fine, but I think at times she was too tough and my father would kind of chafe at the way that she would be too negative. It was as though he tried to balance that with being more positive while still having very high expectations for what he wanted to see done. He tried to look at the potential and possibilities that people have and the positive side of things rather than try to focus on the negative things.

*   *   *

I don't agree with some parents who say I want to be my child's best friend. I think if you go into it with that kind of objective, you're not going to be as effective as you can be. There are going to be times when you're not your child's best friend, you're the parent. At the end of the day, I think there is something to be said for children responding to a parental figure. I would hope that down the road with my kids, I end up offering some advice, guidance or support where I am like a best friend. But certainly that shouldn't be my objective.

*   *   *

I think that certainly for parents of kids who are young, you need to set boundaries. You also need to have kids on a schedule because kids will thrive on a schedule. They know what to expect. I'm amazed at parents whose kids are out late at night and then they're trying to get them up for school. These kids have no concept of what the heck their schedule is all about.

*   *   *

There are so many parents who are well intentioned about trying to help out Johnny or whoever. You know what? Kids need to learn how to fail, and that's a painful thing for a parent to come to grips with. I basically had a pretty damn good life. I can't complain, but a lot of the best lessons I've had were through failure. If you don't learn how to fail, then I don't know how you're going to really learn to succeed.

In fact, I think there was a quote somewhere from Bill Gates about *Success is not a very good teacher. Failure is.* I agree totally with that. I've seen instances of it in our elementary school where a kid forgot her lunch and now the mother was running it in. Let the kids go hungry that day or mooch off their friends, but let them understand that this is an uncomfortable situation because they forgot to bring their lunch. The same thing with homework. Kids have to deal with the consequences of telling the teacher, *I'm sorry, I forgot my homework*, rather than the mother or the father running in their homework assignment. I mean kids, unfortunately, need to learn to fail in a way when it's not life threatening or where it could do harm to somebody else in a big way.

*   *   *

Growing up, I know some families where the father used the belt. My father never did anything like that. I probably only got smacked around once or twice by my dad but it was pretty serious stuff and I knew that I deserved it. My mother had a really thick engagement band and she used to occasionally just give us a whack on the back of the head. And let me tell you, that would get your attention. Not that she had to do it all that often. My view is you should try to avoid that as much as possible because that shows that you're losing control if you get so annoyed that you got to give your kid a whack.

Having said that, I do think that there are some times when it probably is appropriate because it really drives home the point with a young child that is totally out of line. But I do think you got to be very careful as to how you use it. Nobody needs to be abused. But you know people from my generation. There was always a sense of if you were going to do something that was out of line, there was going to be hell to pay with your parents. I don't get the sense this generation of kids really gets that. And I don't know why that's the case. I don't know if it's parents wanting to be too much like their kid's best friend. I do want my kids to respect me and, in some way, to have a little fear for their father. Not to the point where they feel like, *Oh my gosh, he's going to smack me around*. I would never want that, but I think I've been able to actually walk that line.

*   *   *

Go back to the corporal punishment thing for a second. I have formed a theory that there is a role for that, maybe at least early on. Someone told me once that the first smack is for them, the second one is for you. Don't hit them twice. A whack on the rear end when they're little, that suffices. Sometimes I think we have gotten away from that and I think there are some negative repercussions that I am beginning to see where kids have no fear of you because you don't have that in your arsenal so to speak. They feel that's not a card you can play, and if you do, they're going to call the police or complain at school.

*   *   *

178

I think you should try to find the things that you think will impact the child by taking away those privileges to get their attention. I'll give you an example. Our daughter had been a real bear of late with just about everybody in the family but more so my wife and my son in terms of just a nasty attitude. I had discussions with her: *Hey, this is just not acceptable. It's not the way you were raised. It's not the way we deal with people in the family.* We talked about we're a team. *You know, that's not how you deal with people who are on your team and who you love.* It didn't work. I don't know what made me think of it, but all of a sudden I'm walking upstairs and it dawns on me. I just walk in the room and turn on the light and say, *Honey, I'm done talking about the bad behavior. Mom told me about what happened tonight. I want you to take a good look around the room here.* And my daughter had all these stuffed animals and art work and stuff. I said, *Tomorrow when you come home from school, this is all gone. All this stuff, all your art work, the craft stuff you got downstairs, it's all going away and you're going to have to earn it back.* I said, *You'll get food, you'll get clothing, a warm bed. We love you dearly, but all this other stuff is privileged stuff and you're going to have to earn it back.* I mean we took away her blankie and her special stuffed animal. She had these streamers on the outside of her door. And the next morning my wife says, *You want me to take that?* I said, *Absolutely. I want the visual effect when she comes home that it's a different world.*

*   *   *

I love my wife dearly, but she has the unfortunate tendency to say, *Okay, if you do this, this is going to happen,* and then it happens and she will redraw the line. If you tell them to sit down to dinner and they don't want to? Well, my view is, you give them one warning and that's it. Next time, I would just take the plate, wrap it up and say, *Goodnight. You'll be fine. If you're still hungry, get it in the morning.* My kids have seen me in action enough that when I tell them stuff, they know that dad's going to carry through on it. And that's very important.

* * *

We actually have a chart on the refrigerator for each kid. It's got a plastic cover so you can put a marker on it and wipe it off. We keep plusses and minuses. It's a visual thing for the kids to see. We've got to make sure we're noting the plusses, and if there is consistently good behavior, reward that. I think that unfortunately parents generally focus too much on the negative. We all fall into that trap. I do too. But I think you need to be recognizing the positive more.

* * *

I think when they're teenagers, kids should be able to have some degree of independence because you can't keep kids under your thumb for the entire time they're in your house. I mean, that's just not realistic and I don't think you're doing them any favors.

* * *

They need to find their way in terms of standing up for themselves. My kids aren't there yet but they're going to be soon enough. I'm still wrestling with how to make that transition, to allow that transition to happen in a way that doesn't get out of control. I think that kids need to have that. My wife's family didn't have that. God bless my father-in-law. Great guy, love him to death. Passed away a number of years ago. But he was from the tough German school. My wife's siblings didn't have that growing up, and in some respects that was a negative for them because they really didn't learn how to stand up for themselves in situations where they disagree with somebody. They just didn't have that kind of emotional development because they weren't allowed to test the boundaries with their parents in terms of arguing. So again, I'm still trying to figure out how you make that happen. I know

180

how it worked for me and it came out okay, but I do think you got to give kids some room to grow as they're getting to their teens.

*   *   *

If they're still in your house it can be very tough because we've all heard this: *You're living under this house, these are the rules you're under.* Well, you know some kids are eventually going to get to the point and say, *Screw you. I'm out of here.* Is that a good move for them because when they're out on their own then they'll be making even worse choices. I don't know. That's a tough thing. That is a really tough thing.

*   *   *

I know people that have never raised a hand to the kid and it doesn't mean that the kid didn't turn out fine. But I think there needs to absolutely be some kind of punishment that's real, not the timeout that turns into nothing. They're idle threats. I've seen children play their parents because they know their parents are toothless. They're not going to do anything and so they just defy them and do whatever they're going to do.

*   *   *

I think corporal punishment played a role for eons and I'm beginning to recognize there was a legitimate reason for that. It's tougher to do it now because your kids are trained to go complain at school and then they call the cops, and DYFS comes and picks them up, and the police come and handcuff you.

*   *   *

My grandfather used to say that kids are like a sapling. If it starts to grow this way, you put a stake in and you pull it back and they grow straight. If you wait until it's a mature tree that's grown this way, there's no way you're going to change it if you can't move it. There's a fine line. I can remember one situation in raising my kids where I slapped my son across the face and left a hand print on him. I will always regret that. He just pushed me to a certain point, but that was a flaw on my part in not having better control. It was anger. I could have accomplished the same thing without a slap across his face. I could have done it differently. He turned out fine and the mark went away. You can actually do some damage to a child if you're not careful. But I am a firm believer that kids need to be punished and kids need to be disciplined. Some kids are a lot easier than others. There are just kids out there that are absolutely stone headed and obstinate. You know, they're harder. That's all there is to it. They're harder to raise.

*   *   *

From a discipline standpoint, what would be some of the things that we would do? Oh you know, the old, *You don't eat your dinner you don't get a snack. You go to bed without watching TV.* You keep them in, depending upon what age we're talking about. In the younger ages, you punish them by a whack on the butt or *You're not going out to play* or *You're not going to watch television* or *You're not going to get a snack* depending upon what the problem was.

When they're older it's, *You're grounded,* or *You don't get to use the car,* or *You don't get to out this weekend.* That's the best thing you can do at that point. You can't send them to their room because they've got the Wii and they've got the laptop and all kinds of stuff. I can see where depriving them of those technological goodies would be a good way to deal with behavior problems.

*   *   *

Think about what you're trying to accomplish. I learned a

lot from teaching boys. I came out of college and went back to the Catholic school that I went to and all of a sudden I'm sitting there and I got 22 or 23 8th grade adolescents. If you're smart, you realize you're outnumbered. Therefore, be very economical with the word *Yes*, and with the word *No*. Be very economical with threats. If you threaten something, if you're going to maintain order, you're going to have to live up to whatever you threaten. And I think I learned that from my dad, but I definitely used it in maintaining order with groups of kids.

So I used to tell my own adult kids, be careful with *No* and be careful with *Yes*. They're very powerful words. And *Maybe* is acceptable. *Maybe* is an acceptable term stated honestly. You can't use it dishonestly. When you think about that, *I don't know* is acceptable. And I think you get more credibility if you come back and you're honest on that level. Even with a small child. I don't know how frequently I see it in grocery stores. An exasperated parent with a three or four year old. You know, three and four year olds have not yet mastered the art of public behavior. Parents say, *You do that, I'm going to kill you.* You're not going to kill the child. Don't say that. It's an idle threat, which the child is very quick to understand. The next thing you assert is not going to be credible. So stay away from those kinds of broad assertions that are easy to say out of frustration. You're not going to implement them, and you belittle your credibility. Because with raising children, credibility is enormous. Don't let them challenge your credibility. Children are very good game players.

*   *   *

I guess this may not be a good example but it's a good story. We lived next door to a family that has seven kids; five boys, two girls. The oldest boy is in high school. An oak tree on a Saturday jumped into the grill of the high school kid's car and the boy wound up overnight in the hospital. My daughters were probably 10 years old. They ask, *Did you hear that so and so was*

183

overnight in the hospital? I asked them, *You want to go see the car?* I piled my kids in the car. I go around to the place where it's been towed. We got out of the car and there is blood all over the windshield. And there's blood all over the door and all over the handle and all over the front seat. And the front of the car was all bashed in because it was a big oak tree that jumped out in front of him. I didn't give them a lecture. I didn't comment on the boy's behavior. I didn't say negative things. I just looked at it. My kids looked aghast. And there's a lesson. I said, *Alcohol and cars don't mix. And you're old enough to learn this stuff. Alcohol and cars don't mix. I don't care where I am in the world, I will get you home. But do not get behind the wheel of a car when you're drinking. Please. They don't mix. Don't get in the car. I'll get you home. No questions asked.* It wasn't a lecture. It was this great genuine example. And those kids can tell you that story today. I hope they do the same thing with their children. It was a better way to communicate: up close, personal, real.

*   *   *

I'm thinking back again with my twin girls when they had their bikes and it was the summer. I don't know how old they were. We lived about two miles from this little village where there was a spa or something. My daughters said, *Can we ride our bikes to the spa?* And I said, *I don't know. I got to think about that. Give me a minute.* And I went in and talked to my wife and I said, *What do you think? What do you think this decision is going to tell them? Well, if we say yes, we trust their judgment and they're old enough to do that. And say no, it could mean we don't trust their judgment. And they're not old enough to do it.* Ultimately we sat down with them and said, *Okay. Let's go through the risks associated with you riding a bicycle to downtown and back. How are you going to handle the traffic lights? How long are you going to spend down there? How long is it going to take you to get down there? How long is it going to take you to get back?* Serious questions. *Okay. Go ahead.* No cell phones back then. No text messaging. Other parents were mortified that we let our children do that. The way I looked at it, they were old enough to do it. They were quite responsible. And they had quite a good sense about the fact that we let them do that and every other parent wouldn't. And I think it actually increased their sense of responsibility.

*   *   *

It's okay to be critical of the behavior but you need to separate the behavior from the person. If you don't, a child, and an adult for that matter, will have a defensive reaction. *You don't like me. You don't love me. That has nothing to do with that. This is not about whether I like you or I dislike you; whether I love you or I don't love you. This kind of behavior is unacceptable. Let's talk about the behaviors.* And separating them is very hard because you want to call them a melon head. That's what my father used to say.

*   *   *

I think what you want, what you're trying to do in this crazy world, is to give them the judgment to make decisions.

*   *   *

They graduate from high school. They come to me and say, *There's a party in Cape Cod and the whole class is going.* They hand me a form. And they say I need to sign this. I read the form and it's from Mr. and Mrs. Out of their Minds. It says, *Johnny's having a party and we're going to serve booze and we're going to collect all the keys to the cars so nobody can drive. And in order for your child to go, you need to sign this waiver.* And I read it a second time and I ask, *Have you read this? Yeah. You understand it? Yes. You understand that you're asking me to break the law? What do you mean?* And I said, *If I put my name on that, I'm aiding and abetting drinking underage. I know you can drink in this house. I've served you liquor in this house. If I put my name on*

185

that, I'm aiding and abetting them serving you liquor, which is illegal. So this is not about you going to that party; this is about me signing this form. They were absolutely, totally pissed off at me. And they made no bones about it. And I said, *Hey, don't ask me to do anything illegal. Don't ask me to be stupid. That's stupid.*

*   *   *

My first encounter with children was with my nephew who did things like hit people. He was three years old. We're in the kitchen at my house. And his mother had said, *We believe in reasoning. We don't believe in abusing our child.* But this kid is hitting people, including my mom. So he comes over near me and I said, *You got a minute? It's okay to hit people. I'm just trying to point something out to you. Some people hit back, and if they're bigger than you are, it hurts. You got it?* I knew exactly what he was going to do. He hit me. I grabbed him by the wrist and hit him with a knuckle in the arm. Screaming, he runs into the bedroom, tells my brother and his wife that Uncle Dan hit him. My brother comes in with steam coming out of his nostrils. He says, *What'd you do?* I said, *I reasoned with him.* I was on the shit list with my brother and sister-in-law for two years. Honest to God.

As the kid gets older, my brother and his wife realize they don't have a will. They go home and they ask their son, *Of all the relatives in the family, if we weren't here for some tragic reason, where would you like to go?* He said, *I'd like to go live with Uncle Dan.*

I think I made sense to the guy. I go back on my teaching. You've got to establish a predictable pattern for kids. They're constantly pushing the limits. There's got to be stability. There's got to be guidelines. They got to be able to predict. They're still going to challenge you. If you're uneven in your answers: *Yes means yes, yes means no, yes doesn't mean yes,* then you don't have a chance.

186

*　　*　　*

My granddaughters are at an age where they're joining the national debating society. Everything's a negotiation. We're over at my daughter's house and everybody's there. So we've got kid chairs and we've got adult chairs. One of my granddaughters, who's a very striking young lady, decides she wants to sit on an adult chair. And I said, *I don't think so. If you count up the number of people in this room that are adults, and then the number of kids, there are just enough chairs for everybody. I think you ought to get in that chair. No. I'm not moving*, she said. I don't really take well to that from a three year old. And she knows exactly what I'm saying. Not by the words but the inflection in my voice. She slapped me on the left arm. She's in my arms and she's wailing and screaming at the top of her lungs. I take her in a private room. And I look at her and say, *Why are you embarrassing yourself? You can behave this way all you want in here but you're not going to behave in there that way.*

She shut up. And I said, *Do you understand you're embarrassing yourself? Do you see your mother and father behaving that way? They don't behave that way. No adults behave that way. Why would we accept that from you? It's not an option for you.* I said, *Now listen, we're going to go back in there. We're going to act like this didn't happen. So I don't want you to embarrass yourself anymore than you already have. You got it?*

I think it's about creating expectations at a very young age. I think it's much more understandable to say, *Hey, not here. We don't do that here. Do you see anybody doing that here? We don't do that here.* I do not believe in talking down to children. If you want children to understand, talk up to them. Drag them up to your vocabulary.

*　　*　　*

I've always encouraged open discussion with my kids. There was never a sense of, *I'm the parent and you're the child.* And philosophically I've always believed in that. I've always talked to my kids like they were older than they were. There was never, *I'm your father. You need to respect me.* I've never said those words to my kids. I've always felt that I want them to feel comfortable speaking whatever they want to say without fear of getting in trouble for saying anything. When my kids grew up, they were never punished for anything. That was not something I ever believed in. They would get into minor trouble, and as close as they got to being punished was a threat of punishment. And both of them laugh about it today. Not in a mocking way. It's more good-natured, but they once said to friends of ours, *You know, my parents never followed through on a single threat. Not ever. Not one time.* And they laughed. So it was pretty hard to really get in trouble in my house. Even though it was clear violation of rules that you would assume a kid could get in trouble for. School called once and said, *Your son's been reported as leaving school property at lunch time and we're doing an investigation.* I became irate. Not at my son, at the person who called me to waste my time. My position was, *Why are you calling me? What does this have to do with me? Well, your son... it's the rules.* I said, *Well you got to do what you got to do, but I'm not interested.* I said, *If you want to talk to me about where my son goes to college, call me anytime. I'm interested in that, but I'm not interested in this.* When he came home and I relayed the story to him, it was more amusing than anything else.

*   *   *

I always encouraged a healthy disregard for most authority. And I think what that served to do was allow my kids to feel a couple of things. One of them was that I'm intensely loyal to them. Intensely loyal. I've said to a lot of people, and I swear I believe this wholeheartedly, that I take my kids' side 100% of the time. I almost don't need to know the facts. I prefer the facts but it doesn't

188

matter. I'm 100% on their side, and I believe if you do that with your child, you're going to be right 95% of the time. So I always go with them. If a teacher complained, I would attack the teacher. My feeling was always that the greater good is giving your kid a sense of real security through unbelievable and virtually blind loyalty.

I always liked the stories that my kids told me. My son went to Lower Merion High School, a place with a lot of rules, and he liked to break the rules a little bit. I was great with that. I think that's a precursor to good things to come. I never wanted my kids to follow the rules so completely. Why? Because I think it creates a sense of independence and strength to make a decision to break a rule. I don't mean big rules. There are some big rules I don't believe in breaking. But I can actually only think of one: drinking and driving. But other than that, the rest of it never mattered to me, and so a little bit of trouble always made me laugh. When he wasn't supposed to go to his locker at lunchtime but yet he needed to get a book, the hall monitor, whoever that genius was, wouldn't let him go, so he went around the back staircase and got the book and he went, *Hey*, and raised the book up in the air sort of defying her. I was perfectly fine with that. Perfectly fine.

*　　　*　　　*

My sense of successful parenting is measured in only two ways. It certainly works for me. One of them is that you have to give your kids a real good sense of confidence. *I can try things. I'm not afraid to travel to Europe. I'm not afraid to do whatever. I'm willing to take chances. I feel good about my ability to make decisions in life.* That's one. And the second thing is that they want to talk to you. And I think if you get one and two, you get to spike the ball. The idea of, say, *You have to get great grades*, I don't think factors into the equation. Because I don't think you can force any of that. My daughter was a super student and never got anything but an A in school. My son had As and Bs, but the places

189

where he was weaker or didn't apply himself, I don't think I could ever affect, and therefore I think it's a losing battle.

*   *   *

The things that parents punish their kids for - - all things that we did and in my case many times - - are things that I encourage my kids to do. Well, I didn't encourage them, but I didn't discourage them and didn't punish them for it. I think it was good for them to take chances and break some of those rules. And I never punished them for getting in trouble as a result of that. And therefore, because they never got into trouble for anything, they didn't have to lie to me about anything. They weren't going to get in trouble for it. What's the difference? The basic philosophy of not getting in trouble means they'll tell me stuff. And it's just always better to know, particularly in the case of teenagers. If your kids are telling you stuff, and it could be stuff like, *Hey I went to a party and so and so was smoking pot,* man, you're way ahead of the game. Way ahead of the game. Because if you find out that your kid has done something, like breaking out of school and going away at lunch time and he gets in trouble for it, they don't stop doing it. They just stop telling you about it and that's the greater risk. So I always had a pretty good sense of what was going on with them because there was no penalty for anything. So why wouldn't you tell dopey dad? *I'm not going to get in trouble for it. Might as well tell him what's cooking.*

*   *   *

My son was a sophomore in high school. He came home one day and out of the blue he says to me, *Dad. I'm thinking of smoking marijuana.* And we had just a great conversation about it and my argument was, *You don't know a single kid who is both really academic and a great athlete who smokes pot. You can't find that. And right now you're both, so I would tell you that I think it's probably not such a good thing to do.* And I actually staved off that

190

day for a year. I got one year on it, but had I come down really hard on him, I think that I just wouldn't have known about it. Later, he told me when he did it.

What was my reaction then? My first reaction was the safety aspect. I said, *I don't think you're ready yet. I don't think it's such a good idea. Some day you may want to experiment. I understand that. I did in college. So maybe that's the right time for you to get involved.* I said, *When you really want to try it, you can do it here in this house.* And he said, *What?* And I said, *Why not? Of all the places, this is the one safe place. You're here. No one's driving. Nobody's doing anything stupid.* And I think he was sort of surprised by that. That sense of, *Wow. This guy may not be such a bad guy. He's a schmuck sometimes but he's not a bad guy. He gets it.* And both of my kids know that during college, I had my adventures. I don't know that they know the extent of the adventures but I said I did smoke pot in college. They knew I did it as an adult. I knew for sure that they were going to get exposed to it and therefore why set some rule that they, by definition at some point, were going to break?

*   *   *

Be careful when the kids wake up in the morning. Since they're teenagers, they wake up as bears. You really need to stay away from them. Never engage them in conversation until they engage you. That's the first rule.

*   *   *

I figured out that the best way to handle kids, daughters in particular, is using rope-a-dope. Rope-a-dope as in Muhammad Ali. Remember that fight he had? He engaged in a fight with a much stronger man and instead of fighting the fight, he simply protected himself and backed himself up into the ropes with his hands protecting his face and body. He was punched and punched

191

and punched until Foreman punched himself out, and then he won the fight. I think that rope-a-dope is the right way to go with teenagers because they are by nature irrational. They aren't rational people, and to have a rational argument with a person who's not rational is only foolish. So it was better at that moment to let my daughter throw her punches, virtual punches obviously. But throw her punches, and at some point she was going to punch herself out. Then I could get back in and finish the discussion. I used to see it all the time between my wife and my daughter.

A teenage girl spends $150 on a pair of jeans because she had to have them, and the day after she buys them, she hates her pants. What rational argument can you make to convince her that those are the right pants to wear? How can you possibly have that discussion? There's no logic to it. So you sort of let them go and use the rope-a-dope philosophy which I think makes a lot of sense. So I've always felt that if you don't engage them, it's always just a lot better. I mean engage them in discussion but don't go for the fake and start the fight and argue logic. *You just brought them yesterday. You tried them on yesterday. Yesterday you really liked them.* Where's that going to take you? It doesn't go anywhere good. There are no logical arguments and you're going to get back something that makes no sense. So don't argue the point.

So I encourage my wife always to lay back on that stuff. You have to swallow some things that you don't want to swallow. But I do think that the greater good is the relationship, and if you can protect your relationship, you keep them.

*   *   *

Show them respect. And part of respect is listening to what they have to say and accepting the fact that, certainly through their eyes, their ideas and their thoughts are just as good as yours. And you know something, half the time they are. Really, half the time they are. So cursing in my family was allowed. It was okay for a kid to say, *Hey dad. You're being an asshole.* That was fine in my house. That was acceptable. I didn't prefer it, by the way, but it was acceptable. And the truth is, when they accused me of that, they were probably right. So they were simply observing something that was true and expressing themselves. If the kid said to me, *Dad you're being an asshole.* It wasn't like, *Well you're going to be punished the rest of the day*...what for? I was being an asshole. And there were times that I told my son, *You're being a complete asshole here.* That's the way I talked to him. I always felt that he could accept it and take it, and although it sounds bad, in some ways it was very respectful of him.

In other words, we're not exactly peers but we kind of are. I always thought that they made sense. They said things that were smart. They had very good insights. So who says I have the market cornered on wisdom. But I think all of that helped to encourage in them some feeling of respect for me. *He is clearly unconditionally in love with me. I can't do anything completely wrong with him. My worst day with him is going to be a pretty good day. And therefore I feel good about myself.* So my daughter went and climbed Mount Kilimanjaro. I wouldn't do anything like that. Never in a million years would I do anything like that. I wouldn't have had that feeling inside of me that said I could do a thing like that. She's very adventuresome as a result and certainly not afraid to express herself. And further, she would never tolerate somebody not treating her well. Never. I can knock on wood. I never have to worry that a guy that she was dating wasn't treating her well. She wouldn't put up with it for ten seconds. Two seconds.

*   *   *

What about the drinking and driving? It was zero tolerance. Did they believe it? Oh yeah, and the reason I know that is, I used to hear conversations on the phone. My son would be talking in front of us. He would be talking to one of his friends on the phone and I hear this, *No. No. I drove last time. This time it's your turn to drive.* That's a euphemism for I want to drink and you can't. And I was like a lot of other parents. *It doesn't matter. If you're in a situation, you can call me anytime, 24/7. Nothing's going to happen. I'm not going to fight with you. You're not going to be punished.* I really lived those words and, knock on wood, to the best of my knowledge, they never did. But even today, we would go out to dinner and my son will say to me, *Hey, this is your second glass of wine. You think that's a good idea? You have to drive home.* So they demonstrate responsibility. And neither one of my kids is a drug user. They both smoke pot. They both told me about it which doesn't bother me. So for them it was like wearing a seatbelt. Kids don't get into a car without putting on their seatbelt. And drinking and driving is a really bad thing for them. I guess when you only have one rule, that's not so hard. Being able to do almost anything else without any retribution, maybe had something to do with it.

*   *   *

My dad never lost it. He never said, *Son, why did you hit your brother?* Or *Why are you fighting with your brother? You know you could hurt him.* It wasn't like that. It was simply, *You, up in your room. You, I'll see you tomorrow morning. You're in for the night and that's it.* And it wasn't, *But dad...*I don't know if we are more cerebral. What do you call that, hovering parents? We just tend to hover, whereas my dad and my mother were simply, *Here's the way it is.* It was a monologue, not a dialogue. *This is it. You did this. Here are the repercussions.* And you learn not to do it anymore. That style of parenting seems to be lost for whatever reason. It's lost on me, I know that. I tend to want to talk my sons through things or want to over-analyze or over-describe the situation, and that's not always good.

*   *   *

You ever hear of knob hockey? It's this wooden thing you

194

put on the floor and you hit these little wooden sticks and you try to hit it into this little net. Well, we had this, and we had it for an hour. My Uncle Bruce would bring us the best gifts every Christmas Eve in this huge satchel, and he brought in this hockey game. We always had a huge Christmas Eve party and we still do. We were playing it. I was 6 and my brother was 8. And my dad said, *Guys, the house is packed. Put it away. You're going to hit somebody with it.* The next thing I know, boom. I hit my mother in the head with the puck. My dad walked over, grabbed the whole thing, didn't say a word. Just grabbed it, broke it over his knee in the middle of the party and threw it out in the middle of the street. Closed the door and went back to whatever he was doing. That was it. I tell my kids that story. My response would have been, *Alright guys. That's it. The game's on timeout. I want you up in your room. I told you this and here's why. You could have taken an eye out.* Lots of reasoning and explanation. But that's not how it went with my dad.

* * *

I guess the message is telling them versus showing them, or teaching them by doing. This got through to me. I want respect from my kids and I want them to listen to me and to heed me as their dad, not out of fear but out of respect. And for me, it wasn't out of fear. I wasn't afraid of my dad but I respected him. I respected his house.

* * *

My dad was a firm believer in that how we would wind up in life was dictated by who we hung around with as children and what our peer interaction was. Who he would let me hang out with or who he would not let me hang out with was based on his impression of that person. And I truly believe to this day, that that is spot on. They can start hanging out with the wrong crew or doing things that they would never do regardless of you saying, *No*

195

son, that's a bad idea. Our peer choice is crucial to where we wind up in life.

*   *   *

It is in how you say something. My mother - - I really didn't have a father - - used to give me this, *Because I said so.* I made up my mind that I would never say that to my children.

*   *   *

We had ground rules. If the kids were out and were going to be out after 1:00, they had to call us before 11:00. If they were living at home and working, they paid rent. They made their beds every day. If they ate at home, they needed to cook a meal for the family once a week. These rules were not hard to put in place and maintain. And when they came home from college, the rules were still there.

*   *   *

Their friends were always at our house. Through junior high school and high school, the kids were always there. I think they felt at home; this was their home. And the home was an inviting home. I even take it when my kids get snappy with me, which they still do. I take that as a compliment. I feel that it's their way to release. They feel that they can say things to us, and maybe get a little fresh. They feel comfortable and safe with their parents so they can do that. Maybe that's just a rationalization on my part. I say, *Well, they feel comfortable.* They know they're not going to get smacked around or there's not going to be retribution or anything like that. That's fine.

*   *   *

My parents had rules for everything, and I think that by

having rules for everything, it allowed some of the less important things to become more important and some of the more important things to get lost in the shuffle. So one of the things that I have learned is that you need to know when to pick your battles. Which ones are more important? Which ones deserve the attention?

*   *   *

It helped that my wife and I have a great relationship and know how to communicate. We don't agree on everything, but the kids saw that we were on the same page. They knew they couldn't play one of us off the other.

*   *   *

We all want to be liked by our kids. But we also need to be disciplinarians, to make tough calls. You need to set boundaries and rules. One, how the kids interact with and talk to adults and their parents: with respect and never with profanity. Two, they go to school and get good grades. Three, they don't get everything they want. Four, they do chores. You have to insist on rules. Eventually, they will buy in because they will learn right from wrong. They will resist doing what is right, but they at least will know the rules.

*   *   *

My wife is tougher on the kids than I am. She is the bull in the china shop. Zero tolerance. She is on them constantly. I am more willing to listen and ask questions. We had curfews, rules and consequences. We would take away privileges, and one of us would always be up to greet them when they came home. But I wasn't real strict. I had to put them up against the wall a few times when they were disrespectful to my wife, but generally we had the usual teenage issues and not a lot more. Nothing bad happened. Some of it was just dumb luck.

*　　*　　*

I might have been too strict. You want your kids to behave and be respectful. But you don't want them to be nervous, lack confidence, walk on egg shells or always feel they have to ask permission. I have loosened up since they got older. I was more firm, strict and temperamental when they were younger. The tone of the house was too tense. Loosening up means allowing kids to grow up and make decisions on their own.

*　　*　　*

I never had a curfew growing up, and I never gave my daughters one, except on school nights. We would reason with the kids about when they should come home. 3:00? OK. If they were at the late night movie, we would be OK with that and would tell them not to rush home. But if they said they would be home at 2:00, I wanted them to call me if they were 1 minute late because we didn't want to worry.

*　　*　　*

I had zero tolerance for drinking and driving. In fact, I never let them drink at home until they were 21. This was part of teaching them to respect the laws of society. When we went to Cancun, where the drinking age was 18, they could drink. But not at home. And I never gave them permission to drink at college, though I know they did.

*　　*　　*

Kids want discipline. I think my daughter wanted to be told when to come home - - after she was caught drinking underage and had to pay $5,000 in legal and court costs, which drained her bank account. Structure helped her resist peer pressure, which is intense.

* * *

I think you can be as strict as you want as long as at the end of the day, deep down, the kid knows, *My parents love me unconditionally and they'll always be there for me for the important stuff.* I don't want to say then you almost got a free reign to do whatever you want, but I think you can stick with the boundaries you've set. And look, they're not always going to like it. In some cases, they're going to be really annoyed, but I think at the end of the day they will go along with the program even if they don't agree with it because they know deep down, *My parents do love me.*

* * *

Discipline

Questions:

1   *What is your philosophy about disciplining your kids? How does this compare to your spouse's?*

2   *Have you and your spouse reconciled any differences in your philosophies and approaches?*

3   *What rules have you set for your kids? Are these the right ones? Are they clear? Do your kids follow them?*

4   *A lot was said about consistency and follow through. How are you doing with these?*

How Your Kids Describe You

I hope they would say he loved us unconditionally and wanted us to be healthy and well educated, the same aspirations I got from my father.

Someone that they can talk to about virtually anything.

They would say I taught them about right and wrong. That I taught them how to bond with their kids. That even if they drove me crazy, I stilled loved to be with them.

They would say I would do anything for them. That I would take a bullet for them.

I think my kids would describe me as tough. I joke around with Melissa. I say, *Melissa, now that Brittany's going away to school and Chris is away, guess what? You're my only project.* She says, *Oh great.* You know what's funny? On the one hand she says, *Oh no*, cause that means I'm up her butt every night about her homework and stuff. On the other hand, she loves the individual attention. So, I think I would hope that they would say tough, but fair. But also, their biggest fan.

*   *   *

My kids would describe me as patient. I would like to think patient and loving. And I think very consultative and not overbearing. They might also describe me as too easy although I don't think I'm at the 100% mark. I think on that spectrum I might be 70%. I do not let them get away with murder. I do not let them have a million kids over and drink and go crazy. Although I also don't lock them up.

*   *   *

The kneejerk response is I want them to say that their dad loved them unconditionally, but it doesn't matter because I have no expectations of my kids. I have the greatest joy being a father and I also think I'm pretty good at it. I want my kids to be happy. I told my daughter if she ever goes to counseling with her husband, *I give you permission to say anything you want about me because of all of the mistakes that I've made. You should talk to somebody about it.* Sure I want them to know that they're loved. I want them to be happy, but I don't have that need from them. I have needs from my wife, needs from my brother, needs from my dead parents. I still have needs. The only place in my life where ego just disappears is with my kids. The only place that I am at least aware of being egoless. Most of the time.

*   *   *

High expectations would be number one. They probably describe me as very tough. They would describe me as someone who cared very deeply about their welfare. And they both probably say they feel sorry for me because I'm married to their mom.

*   *   *

My daughter just got back from a writer's workshop at Dennison University. The writer's workshop is fiction, non-fiction and poetry. So you can pick one track and then dabble in the other two. She was there on Father's Day. So she sat me down. She said, *I wrote a piece for you. Can I read it? It's for Father's Day.* She was making fun of one of the great family stories. We all went to China in 2005. So we we're driving from Philadelphia to JFK Airport and parking offsite, so I had built, in my typical way, so much time into the process that we were actually at the terminal before it opened. They were still sweeping the floors. And my kids just looked at me. It's like, *Oh my God; I can't believe how early we're here.* My daughter was teasing me in this little piece of writing and then she said, *But you know, dad believes in the commitments that we make. And if we've said that we want to ride horses and we're going to do it on these dates and these times, he believes that we should do it and be there on time to do it.*

So one of the things that they would say is that dad believes that if we make a commitment to something, that we should live up to that. And that was what her poem was about. They teased me endlessly because they know that if the commitment is at 7:30 in the morning that I'll have them there by 7:10. But it was interesting that she was able, at even age 16 to step back and say, *It's not just about being there at 7:10; what he's doing is helping us live up to whatever the commitment is that we've made.*

*   *   *

I hope that they would recognize that I love them all. Both in saying it to them and in supporting what they do. I think they would say, even though my daughter and I have battled over the last two years, that if they chose to do something, that I want to try to be supportive of their choice as opposed to having them have to complete my agenda. I don't have any agenda. I try not to impose my agenda on them or live vicariously through them as I've seen so many soccer parents do. So I'm hoping they would say that whatever they choose to do, that I support them in that effort.

*   *   *

I think they would describe my wife as the poet, the emotional one, the one who is quick to love, quick to get angry, quick to get over that. I'm probably more of the one who's a little more deliberative and not quick to make a decision or a judgment on what they're doing. But it's very interesting that, maybe far more than I knew my own parents, I think all three kids have a pretty good handle on us. They seem like they've got me figured out. It didn't take long. I guess I'm just not that complicated.

*   *   *

I hope they would say he loved us unconditionally and wanted us to be healthy and well educated, the same aspirations I got from my father. And that he was proud of us regardless of what we did as long as we put our effort and care into it. That it didn't make so much difference what we were doing because he would support us in whatever we were doing.

*   *   *

I would assume they would say involved. I'm involved. It's interesting because we go to the school and social stuff. The same parents are involved in everything. The same ones that are involved in leading scout groups are the ones coaching baseball. My wife and I are actively involved in our kids stuff and I think they appreciate that. Both my boys say it's good that I coached. It was good for them, good for me, good for us. I fall asleep a lot because I'm tired. So if we watch a movie, I fall asleep. They would laugh about that, saying, *He's always tired.*

*   *   *

That's a tough question. I would think they would describe me as someone who cares a lot about people, cares a lot about them obviously, a good provider and someone that they can talk to about virtually anything. We haven't had a lack of challenging experiences with the kids in their 20s. And I think they would say I've always been there for them and I think they'd give me a passing grade. Maybe a B+. A- or a B+.

*   *   *

As a jackass probably. You know, I like to think that they look at me as being somebody who's got some of the same qualities my father had. That I've always worked for them. I've always tried to give them better opportunities than I had. Sending them to the private Catholic high schools, sending them to the schools they wanted to go to for college, paying for all of that. Two of them are married and we paid for my daughter's wedding and we paid for half of my son's wedding. It's not just financially. They know that they can rely on me and they can count on me to help them out if they get into a pickle.

*   *   *

I think they would say I was work-obsessed. I did go right back to work in the house for a couple of hours every night. But I was available. I think they would say in certain things, a bit fanatical. I think you should find something that you have in common with your kids…common fanaticism. I think they would both describe me as a really fun dad to have. My kids both liked it when their friends met me. It happened as recently as Monday of this week. My daughter's new boyfriend's friend was going to be in Philadelphia. She said, *You got to meet my dad. He's a great guy.* So I think they would say I'm a really nice guy. I would hope they would both say I'm intensely loyal to them; that I'm their biggest fan, which I am. I mean my wife is a big fan, too, obviously but I'm tied for biggest fan. I think they would say that I'm 100% supportive of them. I guess my son would probably say I can be a pain in the ass sometimes. I can be a pain over small things. Maybe stubborn sometimes. But I think they'd also say that I'm a really good person to talk to and they like talking to me.

*　　*　　*

Fun to be with. Stable. Strict sometimes but generally easy going – more so than my wife who is stricter. Also caring, loving and a good provider.

*　　*　　*

Generally easy going, but the kids know that I can put my foot down and be tough when needed. They also know I can be spontaneous. When, perhaps because I am away with work so much, I try to do some unexpected things with the kids. Like taking my daughter to the airport on a day off. I asked her where she wanted to go. We flew to Boston and had a terrific day.

*　　*　　*

Caring. Concerned. Wanting only the best for them. A strong personality but not overbearing. They would describe my wife the same way. My legacy is my sons. They would say I would do anything for them. That I would take a bullet for them.

*　　*　　*

They would say I taught them about right and wrong. That I taught them how to bond with their kids. That even if they drove me crazy, I stilled loved to be with them.

*　　*　　*

True to my word. Dependable. I'd do anything for them. They would say I helped them get a good start in life. That I didn't ask them to do what I didn't do myself. I think they would say I always supported them.

$$* \qquad * \qquad *$$

Calculating. Caring. Involved – but I always gave them a lot of room. More of a disciplinarian that my wife, who was more involved. Supportive, but firm. Not touchy-feely. I am not buddies with my kids, who are now in their 30s and 40s. They would say I'm reserved but not cold. I am a counselor when they ask, but they need to find their own way.

$$* \qquad * \qquad *$$

Always there for them. They know I sacrificed for them when they were younger. I sent them to private schools, and borrowed money every year to do so. When I made my first bonus, I took the family and my in-laws to Florida. They look back and ask how I did all I did. They appreciate what I have done for them and for others.

Other people would say I did too much for my kids. I don't care. I don't want to be the richest guy in the grave yard. I want to see my kids enjoy the results of my hard work. Why wait till I'm dead? I may be overindulgent, but I haven't spoiled them. I have put them first, spending money on them, not on a boat in the Chesapeake for me.

$$* \qquad * \qquad *$$

They would say I'm stern, work too much, and don't have enough fun. They would say my wife did more to raise them, while I was the provider. Now that my oldest kids have started their own careers, they understand better some of the pressure and stress I

206

experienced when the kids were younger. In fact, I think they appreciate more the job I did as a provider.

*   *   *

They would call me a hard-ass. I pushed some of my kids whom I felt weren't trying to do their best or who wanted to drop out of school. I battled with some of them, and I think they rebelled because I pushed too hard.

*   *   *

My kids would bust my balls when they would see me stressing about work. I don't think they really knew me very well. They didn't understand it was hard for me to leave my "gun and badge" at the office. I have always worried about my job. Ultimately, I couldn't afford to let poor performance impact my role as provider.

*   *   *

There are instances where they probably felt that I didn't listen. But I don't think that they ever felt that we weren't around; that they weren't loved.

*   *   *

How would my son describe me? I think he would say I'm a fun guy to hang around with. I think he would say that I'm smart. I do try to prove to him that I care a lot about people. I will tell him, *I'm in a meeting this morning and it's just to help somebody think through what they would do next in their job. They're struggling with what they want to do next.* But my fear is I just don't want him to be me. I want him to be his own guy and at some point, mold into a better guy than I can ever dream to be.

*   *   *

How our Kids Describe You

Questions:

1   *How would your kids describe you? How would they describe your spouse?*

2   *Why would they describe you in these ways?*

3   *How would you like them to describe you? What would you feel most proud of?*

4   *Are there any changes you should make? If so, will you? How? Starting when?*

Expectations of Your Kids

You've got to demonstrate to your kids that they're good enough. That they're good just the way they are.

Kids need to learn how to solve their own problems and do stuff for themselves. Parents, as well intentioned as they are, are robbing their kids of the ability to be able to problem solve.

You set the rules and the boundaries, but at the end of the day, they have to want it as much for themselves as you want it for them.

Your kids should learn that they need to make decisions, they need to make choices. And that there are rules, and there are consequences to the decisions that they make.

I think we push our kids but we got to let them be who they are, not who we want them to be. I think that's the best advice I can give. You're there to protect them from physical harm and you want to protect them from emotional harm if you can. At the end of the day, you've got to demonstrate to your kids that they're good enough. That they're good just the way they are. And the rest of it is for us; wanting them to be a doctor a lawyer or this or that. You can't. It's easier to see that with your grandchildren than it is with your kids. I see the way some of these kids are raised. Go here, go there, go go go go. I think it's overkill. But that's probably the best advice I can give though it's very difficult to do. When you want certain things for your kids or are telling them to do something, you've got to be conscious of whether you're doing that for yourself, for your own ego, or whether you're really doing it because you love your kid. I think that's a real challenge and a real growth experience to be able to separate the two.

*   *   *

I can tell you about a blessing and a curse. I've learned about personalities. It's what I do and study. My daughter, my 32 year old, has the personality that is geared toward being the best at everything. Whatever she does, it has to be the best. Like the birthday parties for her daughter, running her daycare center; I mean it had to be by far the best in the area. I gave her lots of kudos for her achievements. She achieved a lot early. She knew her ABCs when she was two. I was giving her all kinds of praise for that. I was not the type of father who would be real extreme, like, *Okay let's learn long division because you're now three years old.*

But, on the other hand, I wasn't passive either. I just fed into her desire to please through achieving, and so the curse and the blessing are she knows she can achieve but she never feels that she can achieve enough. Both my wife and I have advanced degrees. And my daughter always felt the pressure of that. No matter how much we said *It's no big deal, we don't care about your grades; learn what you can; have fun,* she got a mixed message. Same thing with my mom. My mom said, *You can do anything you want.* She made me feel like this absolute genius who could do anything, yet I wasn't sure I wanted to hear that.

Hence, I actually dropped out of high school my senior year, and I finished part time six months later because I already had enough credits. I just had to go through the process. I screwed around for three years after high school. Had a job and then went to college; graduated in three years. It was this pendulum of living up to that potential and then backing off, living up, backing off. And so that's what my personality type is...that's a danger for me. I was trying to live up to that. It's taken many, many years to let go of trying to live up to achieve for my mom's sake. It's only been the last few years I feel like I let go. I'm sure it will pop up again somewhere or with something.

It would never have dawned on me that that would be a danger, telling your kids that they can do whatever they want. You think you're bolstering the kid, but you're not.

* * *

My image, my ego I think, is tied to what other people think I can do. As children we begin to learn to satisfy the egos of our parents. So we begin to think that if they're telling us we can do anything we want, then that's what they want for us. They want us to really achieve. Now being happy and truly having the opportunity to do whatever we want is great. By my mom saying I can be anybody I want, she was really saying you could be a doctor, a lawyer, president of the United States. And that was a heavy, heavy dose of achievement. So subconsciously I could never win because I could never live up to her expectation in my own mind. I am 100% positive she loved me regardless. I don't have any doubt in my mind. But subconsciously, this is how my subconscious works; I have to achieve to get her love. That's like coaching a client. I'm not the 'rah rah' coach. I'm the kind of coach that peels back until somebody expresses to me in a clear authentic way what they're about, and then I help them accept that and they feel empowered by that. I try to do that with my kids, too. It's impossible to completely do that because they are always saying, *I better be a baseball fan because my dad loves baseball.*

To me, I want my kids to know without any doubt that they are loved unconditionally. It doesn't matter what they do. I'll support them in whatever they want. Help them get there. Hold their hand. I'll do whatever they need. One thing that they'll always know, no matter what, is I will love them. That's my goal. I don't think any kid actually knows that fully. There's always testing that subconsciously.

How do I convey that? One thing that I do every single night, I say to my kids, *No matter what you do, where you go, I'll always love you and that will never change.* I say, *You know, I love you. I love you no matter what. I'll always love you. It doesn't matter who you are.* My son is real proud when he comes home from baseball. He's a good player. I give him praise for that but I'm careful to let him know that I love him not because he can hit so well. *I love the way you fought. I love the way you are willing to have fun.* Whatever works. But I always tell them over and over again how much that I love them. And I think they do know that. Even my older daughter, the 32 year old. She'll say, *I know. You love me just because.* I hope that's real.

*   *   *

I guide my kids, I discipline them, I teach them, I learn from them. You know, the whole bit. But in the end, I don't need them to do a single thing for me. At least consciously. In my consciousness, I don't need them to do a single thing. What I mean by that is I don't need anything from them for me to continue to love them with all my heart.

*   *   *

They don't have to be a certain way or have a particular outcome or get a certain grade or do their homework for me to love them. I see a lot of people who withdraw love at least to some degree. I don't ever do that. To my knowledge I don't.

*　　*　　*

We had some tough times. My son was not the academic type. I liked the books. That's my thing. This is another lesson that I learned. As long as I had my foot up his ass, he would get good grades. When I removed the foot, the grades would drop down to a C. He was a solid C student. I had to come to the realization that there's something in this world for everybody. Just because you like the books and the academics, everybody's not into that sort of thing.

So I started having a different kind of dialogue with him. When he was in the 9th or 10th grade, the dialogue was along the lines of, *Listen, I can't tell you what to do. You have to figure out what it is that you want to do with your life. You have to figure out what it is that you enjoy doing. Now, me, I enjoy learning and reading and I translate that into something I can use to make money. But if that's not your thing, then that's okay. You can become a basket weaver. You can do whatever you want to do. But understand that you have to choose wisely because you have a certain lifestyle you've grown accustomed to. That lifestyle is based upon what I do. But I won't always be here. You're going to have to get out on your own. So should you choose to become a basket weaver, that's fine. I'm not going to look down on you because you're a basket weaver. But I can tell you that basket weaving will not afford you the kind of lifestyle you've grown accustomed to. Maybe it will, maybe it won't. You've got your thing and you will do well at it.*

And I remember he graduated from high school. He had no intention of going to college and I said, *Okay, that's fine but starting next week, you're going to have to pay rent.* He asked, *What do you mean, pay rent? Oh yeah, you can't live here for free.*

213

If you're not going to college, you have to go out and get a job so you can pay for yourself to live here. And by the way, every six months, I'm going up on the rent. And eventually it's going to get to the point where you're going to be paying market rates for the rent and that's going to hopefully be an inducement for you to want to move out on your own. Because if you can afford to pay the market rate for rent, why would you live under my roof and have to live by my rules when you can go out on your own? That's how we're going to deal with this. He was clenching his teeth. He was hating me. I remember he got a job and he came to me. He just got hired and told me it's going to be another week or two before he got a paycheck. And I said to him, *Well, I'll tell you what. Imagine I called the mortgage company and told them I didn't have my rent or my mortgage. I appreciate your circumstances but all I really need to know is when can I expect a payment. All the trials and tribulations you're going through. I understand it, I appreciate it. You know, those are your issues but I just need to know when can I expect a payment. Oh and by the way, every day that it's late, I'm charging you a late fee.*

That's how we did it. And it eventually got to the point where he moved out. I mean, he moved out on his own and I'm fretting because now I'm thinking, *Man, did I go too far? Was I being too hard? Unintended consequences?* But he moved out on his own and he ended up rooming with this guy. Now listen to this story. This is my son, who grew up in the suburbs. He didn't know anything about the inner city. He roomed with a guy at Broad and Nedro or someplace like that. A really rough neighborhood. And he was sitting there with this guy and the two of them were taking classes at Temple together. They were like two frogs on a log. He told me this story himself. They were talking about, *How did we end up where we are?* So he's describing his story. *I grew up in the suburbs and my father made me pay rent and I didn't want to pay the rent so I left.* The kid looks at him and tells his story. This kid's father is in jail for murder. His mother is a crack head and living and working on the streets, and he's raising his 3 or 4 brothers and sisters while he's working and going to school at night. So that was a wakeup call for my son. Stop feeling sorry for yourself. Get off your ass and do something positive with your life. No matter how bad you think you have it, there's always somebody else who has it ten times worse. You know what I'm saying?

So he ended up coming back home under certain conditions and paying the rent. I actually took the rent and saved it so that when he got married, I gave it back to him as a wedding gift plus some more I put into it to help with a down payment on a house. I told him at that point that it was never about the money. It wasn't about the money. He understands and appreciates that. I remember he called me. I guess he was about 21, 22 years old. He says, *Pop, I found my thing, man.* I said, *Oh what is it?* He says, *It's people. I'm into people. That's my thing.* I said, *Okay, well, go for it.* And that's what he's into, sales. He loves it.

*   *   *

I mean it was tough but I got to tell you, you just never know. That's the other lesson. You just never know. You could do everything perfectly, send them to the best schools; the perfect this, the perfect that; give them this, give them that; do this, do that; expose them to this, expose them to that, and still end up with an axe murderer. And I've seen another situation where these kids have the worst parents in the world and they turn out like jewels. So what is it? I don't know. Is it a turn of fate?

I still can't help thinking and believing that where these kids turn out okay, you'll be able to trace back to some point in their lives when some human being sat them down and talked to them in a different kind of way. To help them to see something in themselves that they couldn't otherwise see without somebody telling them that. Now if you go through life and people are constantly telling you that you're a piece of shit, and everything you see around you is telling you that you're not this, not that, not

215

worth this, not worth that, can't do this, can't do that, eventually, you start to believe it. It's human psychology. But if you're in an environment that's nurturing and caring, you have a chance.

*   *   *

It's tough...by the time they get to be about 13, 14, 15 years old, they have their own lives and there is only so much you can do. You can create the environment. You can set the precedent. You set the rules and the boundaries, but the end of the day, they have to want it as much for themselves as you want it for them.

*   *   *

I started out kicking ass and all that kind of stuff. By the time he was in 9th or 10th grade, I started backing off and saying, *Look, these are the requirements, these are the boundaries. These are the things I know you've grown accustomed to and the things that you want to do and continue to. But other than food, clothing and shelter, the things that I'm legally required to do, you're not getting any extra unless and until you deliver the goods. And that means passing grades in all your courses, period. I'm not going to monitor you. It's on you. I'm going to look at the report card when it comes in and if you make it, that's fine. If you don't, I'm just taking stuff away.*

*   *   *

There were things that he wanted. You take it away. You know there are different buttons that you have to push. A lot of these things like the phones - - the things that they need in order to enjoy the kind of lifestyle that they're accustomed to, but not stuff they have to have to survive. You don't need a phone. You don't need this, that and the other. You don't need to go out on Fridays and Saturdays and do all these kinds of things. Just put a stop to it.

That's all you got. They're too old for you to beat their asses. In fact, the ass whipping needs to stop by the time they're still pretty young. When I say ass whipping I mean, not like beating them like when you and I were growing up. You got your ass whipped. So did I. But you can't do that these days. By the time my daughter was 3 years old, that might have been the last time she had a spanking. Maybe the first and last. I never had to do anything like that. I think with my son, it was a little longer. By the time he was 11, 12, 13 years old, we didn't have to get into anything physical. But that was it. I said, *Listen, if you don't make it into college, in order for you to stay here, you're going to have to get a job and work and pay rent. I don't care what you do, you're getting a job and you're going to pay something while you're here.*

*   *   *

You want your kids to be happy and this is important in terms of how you would define what you want your kids to be. To be happy, to be happy with what they do, be financially independent, and then have attributes like integrity and honesty.

You know, in my house, you better not say any racist statement. No ethnic slurs or anything like that. You know when Barrack Obama gave that speech about race and talked about some people in your family, your extended family, that have strong feelings about race. I do. I got a nephew who's got all these tattoos. He's like 6'4" and the things that come out of his mouth. I had to tell him. I said, *Hey, I don't want to hear that. You can't talk like that around me. I don't think it's good for you either.*

*   *   *

What if my kids were not motivated? Would I be one of those guys beating their brains in to be motivated? I think my son had a chance to just play along and be part of the pack. I forced

217

him. He didn't even know what I was doing. He was in third grade. I put him in a different school with a more rigorous program. I don't think I could accept my kids not being motivated to achieve. I want my kids to have great careers and work hard and be passionate about something.

*   *   *

I think our kids would describe me as being really hugely supportive but tough. You know, we were tough. Our kids had a privileged lifestyle because they were the children of diplomats. But we didn't want them to become the diplo-brats that so many of our colleagues became. And so we would drive them. There were rules. We would make sure that even in a place like India, where we had more household staff than you could shake a stick at, they had jobs to do. They cleared the table. They made their own beds. The adults were in charge. They weren't in charge if we were not there.

They are all successes. They developed an extraordinary work ethic and I think that that's what carries them through to their success. That was something that my wife and I really wanted to instill in the kids. I think they would agree that we were incredibly supportive parents and we are very loving parents but we were tough. That meant that if they hurt themselves, it's life. We said, *Well, you just have to suck it up. This is the harshness of life. Sorry, but this is the real world and you're not going to have us to always support you. You just have to suck it up.*

*   *   *

My son is in London. He's working incredible hours. He works from probably 8:30 in the morning to about 1:30, 2:30 in the morning; five nights a week. He has very little money. We do financially support him, but there's a limit to that because it's his choice to live in London for his career. I said to him, *While you're building your career, we'll support you financially. But if you're*

218

doing it as a semi-holiday, then we're not. So there's a degree of toughness and he recognizes that. There are also the lessons we all learned from our other son's illness which was prolonged and very difficult. He went through enormous pain and all that chemotherapy. You learn that degree of toughness, and there are times when you had no choice but to just deal with it. The kids had that through their lives. They saw people being killed. They've seen mass poverty and we've taught them to appreciate what they have and to help other people when they can. That's an important part of having that more privileged lifestyle.

*   *   *

On my wife's side, she was an only child. Her parents had her when they were very old, particularly in those days. They were nurturing to the point of being smothering. It's interesting. My wife and I sat down when our kids were born and we had a very intellectual discussion about how we wanted to raise our children. I know this sounds really anal, but we basically developed a list of what we wanted. I talked about my father working hard and what I learned from that, and how we had chores to do around the house and we had to do them. Again, you had to suck it up. You had no choice but to do your chores. And so I thought that was a good thing because it taught me how to work hard and that I had to work to achieve what I wanted.

My wife's side was love and nurturing and that's not something I was used to. Her mother used to insist on giving me a kiss every time I walked in the door. My mother never kissed me. I mean, it just never happened. So it was really alien to me and I found it smothering to an extent. We agreed the path was in the middle. We had to be nurturing but we couldn't always protect our children from the realities of the world. And so we would expose them to real life. So that was the middle path that we chose, and I think that was a large part of our success.

I remember talking to my son when he had children. He said he thought his upbringing was magnificent. And he said that's what he wanted to repeat. We've had a number of people who have said to us that our children are so well balanced. Such self-confident individuals. And they ask how we did it. We talked about that and some of the basic rules. You know how many people use the 1-2-3 rule. *I'm going to count to three if you don't stop what you're doing...* And we'd do that 1-2-3 and if we got to three, all hell would break loose. So we actually carried it through. My older brother has this child. He's just the brat child from hell. They count over and over but he doesn't stop because they don't carry through with it. And so it's ineffectual. It doesn't work at all.

*   *   *

Your kids should learn that they need to make decisions, they need to make choices. There are rules and there are consequences to the decisions that they make. That was something we reinforced with them all the time and even do now. Some people probably thought we were too tough. We had a thing about making sure that the kids had the basics in life to survive because we had such a small family. Both of our parents had died early. We don't have any extended families so it's really just the four of us and we'd been living overseas. So we instituted a shit load of process where the kids did their own washing. They cooked a meal once a week. They had to balance a budget. My wife told them if they can cook, clean, and balance a budget, they've got the basics in life. If something happened to us, they're not going to completely fall apart.

So we did that. And so from the time they were quite young, they became self sufficient. So as a result, when our younger son, for instance, was 16, he travelled to Vietnam with his girlfriend and he was fine. And our older son, when he was 16, went to Peru and climbed the Machu Picchu trail. So hugely adventurous, but the most confident international travelers you can imagine as well. Being self-reliant and confident is really important. But they always knew we were there to catch them if they needed it.

*   *   *

My wife and I were young. We recognized the huge differences in how we were each raised and we decided to take this sort of analytic approach of what did and what didn't work. We had such vastly different backgrounds. My in-laws just doted on my fiancé. You walked in the house and there were so many photos of her. It looked like some kind of shrine. It was just extraordinary the devotion they had to her and it became somewhat smothering. It was also very quiet because it was just the three of them when they had dinners.

And then she came to my house for dinner when we were dating and it was just chaos. It was raucous because we were all very strong individuals. When dad was drunk and violent, we would fight back. We never gave into that sort of crap. But even when he wasn't drunk and he was being good, we were still an argumentative family. We would have political discussions because they were all right wing fascists almost. I was the left winger. I was the radical. My rebellion against my parents was to go to the center of town and hand out the communist newspaper. I wasn't a communist, but I just did it to irritate my parents, which worked. But you know, we would have these great philosophical discussions and everybody would be talking over each other. Dinner time was when we would get together and we would have these fantastic discussions over the meal. And my fiancé walked in to this and she was just reeling from the experience from the first minute. She said she never heard such a level of noise in one room in her entire life. She was intimidated at first but as she got used to it, she reveled in it.

So one of the things we put on the positive side was meal

times. We decided we would sit around the table without an external distraction like a television. This is critical to being a family because that's when you talk about your day. You talk about what's happening in the world and you have that intellectual interaction with your children. Whether they're 5 or they're 15 or they're 25. That's the time you talk. That raucous discussion was more or less a fight in our family, but that was our time. So that was on the plus side for my family. On the plus side from her family was the fact that we would actually be demonstrative in our love. So I would say to the kids that I loved them. My father never said that to me in my entire life that I can recall. It wasn't that he didn't because I know he did. They just weren't demonstrative because that wasn't their upbringing. My mother grew up in an orphanage so she never heard that. But I know my parents loved me.

So on the list was that we wanted to be more demonstrative. Later when our son was dying, that became very important to us. There's nothing wrong with telling kids how important they are on a regular basis, not just at Christmas or birthdays. My wife was very protected from life, and when she started going out with me and she saw the harshness of life with my father and all those sorts of things, she said, *This is the real world*. And so again, that was part of the discussion. We would not shield them completely from the real world.

*   *   *

We decided to be tougher, and I can give you an example of that. My wife did not swim, and in Australia it's really dangerous not to be able to do that because everyone swims. The water is a major part of Australian culture whether it's the beach or the pool. My kids not being able to swim was just not acceptable to me. My wife's first instincts were to protect the kids from danger, from water. I said that's actually more dangerous. So when our kids were 11 months old, they could paddle to the side of the pool because I just threw them in the pool. Obviously in a safe environment but by 11 months our kids could jump in the pool and swim to the side, even though they could barely walk. These became our guiding principles for the rest of our child raising.

*   *   *

Teach them how to prioritize. That doesn't come naturally to people. But we do it by asking questions. Or I did when I was on my game by asking questions. My son was a hockey nut in the first grade. Playing hockey is not a sport, it's a disease. He was in school and I said, *Dan, what do you think your priorities are?* He asked, *What do you mean?* He's in third or fourth grade. *What do you think is the most important thing? Getting my work done in school and doing well. Okay. What's the most important thing in your personal life? Hockey. Okay. What do you think is going to go if don't do well in school? Hockey.* Simultaneous with that conversation, he's in a time management class at school that I couldn't say enough good things about. He's carrying around a daily planner. I look at it one day. He's got all of his hockey games, all of his hockey practices and when he's going to study in the daily planner a month ahead. Fourth grade. Was in sports all through high school. Plays on a hockey team at high school and travels with the team. Prioritization. What are their priorities? It's unclear today because the kids seem to be so busy and there's so much going on. There's so many things for them to do. Well, ask. *What are your priorities? What's most important? What's second? What's third?* These are great questions.

*   *   *

I used to coach the kids in soccer. I used to have the parents and kids join together. I'd say that we're going to learn how to win. We're also going to learn how to lose. Learn how to tie. I would ask, *What are the priorities for me as a coach?* I would say, *There's only one negative thing that will evoke my anger and that*

223

is if somebody on this field criticizes a goalie on our team. I said, *You're out of the game with that attitude for the rest of the game.* I told them that, before a goalie has a chance to make a mistake, ten other people have made a mistake. *Goalies should never see a shot in the perfect soccer game. Shouldn't happen. So you've all made a mistake before the goalie even gets a shot at a mistake.* And who am I talking to? I'm talking to the parents because they could be so mean. What priorities are they setting? Win at all costs. They don't mean to be setting those priorities but that's what they're doing. You know, a kid makes a good pass on the opponent's team. I'm coaching. I look at him and say, *That's a great pass. That is a terrific play you just made.* The parents ask, *What are you coaching the other team for?*

*   *   *

I tell her that as you get older the competition gets better and better. If she decided that her passion is going to be playing guitar or writing a book or whatever it is, I would fully support her. But you know, I remind her she really needs to develop habits to work hard because talent alone isn't going to be sufficient.

*   *   *

I think we showed them at every step of the way that we cared about them; that everything they do matters; it matter to us; it matters to other people; it matters to the world. Being responsible. Whether it's being responsible citizens; whether it's being responsible charitable people. I mean giving your time, giving your talents. We've had some of these discussions with the younger guys especially. *You're smart. You can't just not use the talent that God gave you. You have to use it.* So I think it's just telling them every step of the way that we care, and we're willing to support them, and nobody's perfect, and you get forgiven for things that you do wrong that you have a chance to make right. As long as you want to make it right and you want to try better and try harder and

224

do better. While it's not unconditional love, they know that they've got a lot of love and support.

Why is it not unconditional? I don't think I would be the kind of person that if my kid just decided to be a complete and total bum, treat other people like crap, not care about himself or anybody else... Maybe love is not the word. I would just not like that person. I would love him even though I didn't like him. I would not be able to sit by and say, *It's okay for you to be a complete and total loser even though you've had all these opportunities handed to you. It's not okay for you to just not care about yourself or other people.* Maybe that's the issue. I wouldn't overly nurture or support somebody who I knew was bilking the system and not giving it any kind of effort. I don't really think any of my kids are going to fall to that category. I think my youngest son has shown the possibility of having some of that. But when I step back, he's not getting tattoos all up and down and he doesn't have holes in his body and crazy stuff like that. He doesn't have all kinds of really bad stuff going on. He's just a little different than the mainstream people that we pretty much built up.

*   *   *

Let them learn how to go to sleep. In fact, one of the best lessons kids can learn at an early age is that they can put themselves to sleep. And it is the toughest thing to do as a parent, when you hear that kid crying, to not go back in there and pick them up because kids will learn habits like that. You do it that night, then the next night they'll be doing the same darn thing because they know mom's coming in or dad's coming in. Now you have to know your kid, but and I can tell you there were nights where you're looking at the watch. It's only five minutes but it seems like an eternity. You're like, *No don't go up there.* Literally at the 10½ minute mark all of a sudden it stopped. They're gone for the night. The interesting thing is as the kids got older, like three, four, five, and six and maybe they're starting to get into the dream stuff about monsters and what not, it is so easy to go back to that mode. And I would say this to the kids every night: *You know what? You've been a great sleeper every since you were a baby and you are a great sleeper now.* They'd say, *Dad, stay up here.* I'd say, *You don't need me up here because you know how to put yourself to sleep.*

I can't tell you the number of times the kids wanted to suck you in, but you can't do it. And you know what, they go to sleep. As subtle as it seems, kids need to learn how to feel like they can solve their own problems and do stuff for themselves. Parents, as well intentioned as they are, are robbing their kids of the ability to be able to problem solve, and some of it's at a very basic level. Just in terms of taking care of yourself and getting yourself to sleep.

*   *   *

One of the things we've done with our kids, if they're lollygagging around in the morning and they end up missing the bus, my wife charges them five bucks to drive them to school. And they know it. They had to dig down in their piggy bank and take out money and give it to mom. It happened a few times, but basically it hasn't been a problem since. You have to set boundaries, expectations that they know. There's no question. Follow through is critical because kids are very adept at sensing a weakness and exploiting it, and my guess is that goes on right up through the teenage years. In fact, they probably get more astute on how to play those games with parents.

*   *   *

Responsibility is an issue you need transfer to your kids. I believe that children can be responsible but you need to give them the opportunity to be responsible. I wonder at times. I look at freshman orientation in college. Horrible. The kid can't get the class he wants, gets his mother on the cell phone. Hands the cell

226

phone to the registrar. Yikes, look at that kid! Wait a minute. Time out. It's fundamental decision making. How do you teach your children to make decisions? They're making them at an earlier age, including the bigger decisions that they make: booze, drugs, sex. They were made earlier by my children than by me, and they're probably being made earlier again by kids younger than my children.

So my philosophy was, give them a framework for decision making. You have to give them responsibility. And they have to understand it. Maybe I was lucky. I'm sure that I had my moments when they were growing up, but they gave us very, very little pain. I think all three of them are very responsible. They continue to be very responsible people. I think they understood that we were trusting them a great deal. My daughter comes home. She's 14 years old. She has her first boyfriend. I get a call from his mother who wants my daughter to come over to Europe for the summer. My wife and I discuss it. Okay. What are the ramifications if we say yes? What are the ramifications if we said no? She went.

*   *   *

My two daughters went to live in Europe for five weeks and played on an all girls soccer team. Played in Denmark and Holland and trained every day. And they played against 35 year old women. When they were invited to go, they were 15 and they were very comfortable coming to us to discuss it with us. They asked, *What do you think.* And I asked them, *What do you think? What are the pros? What are the cons? What are the plusses? What are the minuses? What might you encounter? How are you going to handle it?* I wanted it to be their decision. *Okay, you want to go, go. I'll pay for it and I just want you to maximize the time that you're there. I want you to optimize the opportunity.* So I think I had this construct of trust. They know at some point in time, it is their life. And I had that relatively early. And I tried to operate in that style.

227

*   *   *

I love my parents dearly but I had the strange ability to be able to look at things that I didn't think were good and say, *You know what? I'm going to do it better. I don't want to be that way. I'm going to do it better.* That didn't diminish my love for them. I think that that's healthy because at the end of the day, nobody's perfect. I don't want any of my kids worshipping me, because I'm not perfect. And I would hope that the things that I haven't done well, they will look at and say, *You know what? I love dad dearly but I'm not going to do certain things the way he did.*

*   *   *

Expectations of Your Kids

Questions:

1   *What expectations do you have for your kids? How will these change over time vs. staying the same?*

2   *How well and how consistently have you communicated these expectations?*

3   *Are your kids clear on these expectations? Do they know what they need to do to fulfill them?*

4   *Does your spouse have expectations that are different from yours? If so, do you need to work on these differences?*

Some Additional Perspectives

Defy the conventional wisdom about how your kids are going to be when they're X age. You decide what you want your kids to be.... And to hell with everybody else that says what they're going to be.

When I was handed my son, I felt this unbelievable sense of responsibility.... It was huge, the most life changing experience that you can have.

We face hundreds of decisions every single day, and I think I come out on the right side of those more often now than I did before just because of [my son]. There's just this aspect of having to face him. It's that cycle of trust. Once it's broken? I'm sure he'll give me a free pass, but I don't want to take that free pass. I just have this fear of losing position in his life, in his eyes.

Absolutely I would show my weaknesses. I'd say to them, *Jesus, I screwed up at work today. Did I make a big mistake! Just from my own bad judgment.* Talking around the dinner table. They learned from that. And they would engage in the discussion. *Well, did you do this? How did you fix it then?* This was from a relatively young age.

*   *   *

One of the things that I found useful was to reject the conventional wisdom about how your kids are going to turn out. I used to hear my friends say, *Wait till they're teenagers. They're going to hate your guts. Wait till they're 16 and they don't want to be seen with you. Wait till they're a junior in high school, they're going to come home drunk. Wait until they go away to college; when they come back home, they're going to hate being there.* It was pretty consistent among a small group of guys who, by the way, don't necessarily have bad kids. But as a group they would say, *That's just the way it is.* I was never very good at having people say to me, *You're only 40. Wait till you're 50.* I was like, *What makes you think you're right?*

I enjoy defying the conventional wisdom, particularly about my kids. I was actually a bit offended that someone would tell me how my kid was going to turn out. And so I find a lot of parents just go with the flow because they think it's inevitable. Like you know, *Your kids are going to yell at you and yell at each other.* Well, we don't yell at each other. We don't yell at each other, period. So anyway, defy the conventional wisdom about how your kids are going to be when they're X age. You decide what you want your kids to be at X age. And to hell with everybody else that says what they're going to be.

*   *   *

Don't listen to everybody else's bullshit. That's the biggest thing. That conventional wisdom is bullshit. I'll put it another way. One of our neighbors, their kids are out of control. My daughter is best friends with their daughter. She comes home one day and says, *Dad, I can't go over there anymore.* I ask why. She said *They yell at each other all the time and the language they use is awful.* Now they're not bad people, but it's the way they converse with each other. That lady is now doing counseling for parenting classes. I think, *Jesus, she's the worst parent I know.* But she thinks she's the best.

The point is, in my personal experience, the people who are the best parents do so quietly. And the ones who have the worst advice are the ones that are most vocal. And so you can be caught in the trap of listening to the vocal minority and believing what they tell you is true. The people whose kids don't hate them when they are 15, don't come and tell you, *Hey my kid loves me and he's 15.* It's the people whose kids hate them when they're 15 who say, *Your kids are going to hate you when they're 15,* because they don't like what happened to them. So they project it to other people.

The only advice you get as a parent is from the people who aren't happy with what they've done. That's perverse to me. So don't follow the conventional wisdom. Don't read a bunch of books, in spite of the fact that you're writing one.

*   *   *

My kids see where I grew up. They understand how I was raised and how I grew up -- what I had, what I didn't have -- and so they appreciate it. At least intellectually. There's nothing like experience. They also appreciate that I'm very different from all of their friends' parents. I don't fit the mold of where we live.

*   *   *

Knowing how hard to push. Letting them fail, which is a hard thing to do. Making sure that they're responsible. We're always concerned about them being "spoiled". It was a challenge coming up with chores for the kids to do because we have someone who makes their lunch, makes them dinner. And someone else who cuts the grass and rakes the leaves and does the laundry. It's the nature of a two-working parent household, so in that environment, how do you ensure that they value what they have and maintain the right values? It's hard. We struggle with that. I know my kids are spoiled despite every conscious effort to the contrary. I hear a lot of my peers complaining about the same thing. We tried not to spoil them but we know they are. Even people with lesser means will complain about it.

*   *   *

She's 25 years old and she has no desire to be tied down. She was dating that one guy that I was talking about, Mr. Life Force. I despised him with a passion, I really did, and I was right. Six months it lasted and that was the end of that. I know a guy who said he deliberately fell in love with every boy his girls brought home, even if he despised the guy, because he felt he would have a son-in-law if he pushed back and said, *This guy's a loser.* Now, take Mr. Life Force. Did she know I didn't like the guy? She absolutely knew it. I didn't hold back.

I'm not going to play that game. I'm not going to take a chance on that game. I feel honestly that she respects us enough and it would help her to open her eyes. When he first came around, he was just kind of abrasive and we were a little put off by him. The second time he came around, we tried to get to know him. After a couple of months we had a talk with her. We asked, *What is it? Help us to understand what you like about this guy because we don't see it. We don't think he treats you particularly well. We don't think he shows that he's got a lot of respect for your intelligence and individuality. He just seems like a very opinionated, abrasive individual.*

*   *   *

We never said, *If you stay with this guy we're going to write you off forever.* It's more, *I don't like him. Here are the reasons I don't like him. Tell me what you like about him. Help me see what I'm not seeing. Family is important to you, so help me understand why some of your siblings don't like him.* He was just a self centered person and...she came to the same conclusion. Actually she was up in New York at a bar. She was talking to some other guy, and the boyfriend went crazy and they went out and had a fight outside. And she called my wife and said, *That's it.* They had just broken up and she said they'd had five of these yelling matches in the last two months. And my wife said, *Wow, that's a red flag.* So they broke up, which was good.

*   *   *

I said, *There's only one sentence you can't use with me. "I can't do it" is not acceptable. That's the only thing I won't accept from you.*

*   *   *

My son is 9. I'll say, *If I'm not doing it right, you let me know. If I'm talking to you in a way that you don't want to be talked to, you let me know and we'll try a different way.* I would say I'm learning a lot from him. How he interacts with his friends. How nice this kid is. How loving he is with his grandparents. I know I should have more of that characteristic in me. You know, I interact with a lot of people at a different level, but not at that deep loving level, which he extends to most everybody. I think that part I try to learn. I think he gives everybody the benefit of the doubt, that everybody's a great person till they prove otherwise 5 or 6 times. I'm not that way. I do see things in him that amaze me. I try to be a little more loving around my brothers and sisters. Hug them when I see them now.

*   *   *

233

With my son, I'm not going to define the agenda every single day. If there are some things that he wants to do, we'll go that way. So it's not like we wake up on Saturday and here are the 8 things I want to accomplish today. I do leave a lot of room for what he wants to do and when he wants to do it. Just like a friend would. I'm not good at controlling this relationship all the way.

*　　*　　*

He has a regulating effect over me. My wife doesn't regulate me internally as much as my son does. It's one of those things where if I ever really screwed up, would I want to go in front of him and have to explain to him what I did and why I did it? My wife, I think, I can get away with that. But with him, I just wouldn't want to do it. We're together so much. We have this great relationship. It's almost this tall guy with this little shadow behind me, but I think the shadow also hangs with me when he's not there. He really does help me think through situations and make better decisions because I don't want to have to face him with making a bad decision.

And we face hundreds of decisions every single day, and I think I come out on the right side of those more often now than I did before just because of him. There's just this aspect of having to face him. It's that cycle of trust. Once it's broken? I'm sure he'll give me a free pass, but I don't want to take that free pass. I just have this fear of losing position in his life, in his eyes.

*　　*　　*

There is a regret I have. I was married before and I haven't shared that with my son. I don't know when or how or if I need to share that, but I think it's going to be one of those things that I have to deal with. I thought about that a lot and it's going to be interesting. I don't know if it's going to be a tough conversation, but I feel like I'm keeping something from him. I have this secret, yet I'm trying to say, *Be honest, be truthful about everything.* I feel like there's this one thing that's hanging out there. It's just never come up in conversation. I think the underlying part of that regret is that I do feel like I share most things with him, and that's a big one that I haven't.

*   *   *

When I was handed my son, I felt this unbelievable sense of responsibility. It was huge and, my God, did it pull me out of being like every other 20 year old who was having a good time and partying. It made me more serious about life. And much more analytical about my own life and what I wanted from my children and everything else. It was huge, the most life changing experience that you can have, and I think everyone would agree.

*   *   *

I wrote something for my parents, called "Parent to Parent," after we had our first daughter. We didn't have kids until a bit later on. I wrote about what my parents, I had learned, gave to my siblings and me. I described four gifts that they gave us, but I didn't appreciate these until I was a parent. The first was just unconditional love. We could have done anything, we could have been murderers, and they still would have loved us. And I thought about what a precious thing that is to have; for a kid to realize that his parents are going to love him regardless of what happens. The second was a sense of right and wrong. Growing up I thought they were too strict. My dad was one of those guys who saw black and white. Not a lot of gray. *This is the right thing to do. You know that. No bullshit. Don't try to talk your way out of it.* Another was the sense of religion and God. It wasn't by beating us over the head. It was just by their own example that they said there's something else out there that is bigger than us and is very important. They left it up to us in terms of what we did with it. The fourth was the sacrifice that they made for us. They should have

235

done more for each other and more for themselves. But the kids came first.

I thanked my parents for these gifts, and I told them I hoped to pass the same ones onto my kids. My mother was very touched by what I wrote and said she wanted to be buried with it. My father never said a word, but I think he was touched too.

*   *   *

My daughter was home for the summer from college. There was a family party down the shore. I learned that my daughter was planning to ride down on the back of her boyfriend's motorcycle. When I learned that I said, *I don't want you doing that.* She said, *Why?* I told her, *You can drive or I'll drive or I'll pay for your gas but I don't want you riding on a bike.* It led to a big fight. She was livid. She pushed me, and I thought her boyfriend, who was there, might join in and get physical. But I said, *No way.* After tears, cursing, threats and yelling, she complied. They drove in a car.

*   *   *

I've seen cases where parents can't say no. We went over to Helsinki, Finland on a soccer tour with my daughter's team to play for the "Helsinki Cup." The kids were 14 or 15. We went over with the coaches and some other family members. When we arrived to the soccer field for the first game, we see signs for the "Helsinki Cup Disco" posted all over the place. This was left unspoken for a couple of days until it came up at a team meeting. The kids had, unbeknownst to their parents or the coaches, decided they were indeed going to go to the Helsinki Cup Disco. The advice we got from our Finnish host, whose daughter was playing on our team, was, *Don't go near this thing. We don't know much about it. We're pretty sure it's for older kids and there will be adults there. They'll be heavy drinking. Let's stay away.* Having heard this advice, the coach calls a parents' meeting. His

236

recommendation to the parents was that the girls not go, but he wanted to make sure that the parents were on board. I was one of the first to speak. I said, *Coaches decide these things, even at a professional level. We're going to listen to the coach. You've decided. This is your decision, and we will abide by it.* But that didn't fly with a couple of the parents. They wanted to let their kids go. They said, *The girls are going to be disappointed. What are we going to say to them?* I said, *Here's a word: No.* It was like the first time they were hearing that. It was weird. The girls didn't go. But unfortunately the dynamics among the coaches, parents and the girls were bad for the rest of the trip.

*   *   *

That's been a struggle with my wife as we raise our kids. We saw examples early on where parents failed when they were too strict, where parents broke the spirit of their kids. The kids didn't have confidence. I've also seen parents fail by being too lenient. The kids go wild and they have no roots. There's nothing that anchors them to a value system that would influence how they behave. So we always felt that you can err in either direction, and that there needs to be a balance. But there's no prescription as to where that balance is. You kind of wing it. You roll the dice. You draw on what you've learned. You pray. You do the very best you can. But there's no guarantee as to being able to find that balance.

*   *   *

I was watching a soccer game with pee wee kids. I think they were 7. Each team had one good player, and they were essentially playing against each other. They were the ones going up and down, up and down...and the rest of the kids were just running around in a pack behind them. There was one father on the sideline who was screaming at his kid. I thought for sure that his son must be one of the two stars. Because these two kids were going at it aggressively, I thought that the father had somehow gotten wrapped up in it. But he was way over the top. Very loud and angry.

At half time he calls his son over. It wasn't one of the two good kids. It was just this little tiny kid who was in the pack of the other kids running around. He's bawling this kid out. He yells, *What are you thinking? What are you doing?* The kid is crying. The little kid looks like a whipped dog. I felt like punching the father.

*   *   *

My two daughters were pretty athletic. They did karate, they did soccer. I tried to get them interested in golf. They would have no parts of it. They would say, *Dad you don't get. It's not that we don't like golf. We hate golf.* Well, my older daughter was a sophomore at Purdue. She gave me a call when she picked up her football tickets. With the tickets came a voucher for a round of golf on the university course. She says, *How about you come out for a weekend. We'll go to the game on Saturday and then we'll play golf on Sunday.* This was the girl who always was busting my chops about golf being a dumb sport. So that's what I did. I couldn't resist. I was very touched. We had a blast. We had dinner Friday night with a bunch of her friends. Went to the game on Saturday; did a little tailgating, throwing the football around, and then we went and played golf on Sunday. It was her first time playing golf and she did extraordinarily well. We had a great time. I'll never forget it.

*   *   *

My wife and I have always said, if my daughter only studied harder, if she only applied herself, if she only would read, if she would only get started earlier on her assignments and things like that, then she could get As instead of Bs. One of the struggles we have as a couple is knowing how far we push that. On the one hand, helping your kids understand that they need to try to achieve, not be lazy, and work hard, are good life lessons. On the other hand, we can push so hard that we make her miserable or give her a sense that mom and dad are only interested in grades. Where's the balance? On the one hand, if we don't push, maybe there's a role that we're not fulfilling that we need to fulfill. But if we push too hard we know that there's a danger of her just shutting us off. There are a lot of things in parenting like this. You can go too far. Or you can not go far enough.

*   *   *

I always thought it was tragic that kids often don't get to know their grandparents as people. My father's parents were immigrants from Ireland. I wish I could have listened to their stories, but we kids were too young to do that. When I was a kid, my grandfather was a scary, austere guy who wore a suit and tie every day, wouldn't say a whole lot, drank Papst and seemed humorless. And then later in life I heard stories about some of the wild stuff that he did when he was younger. I wish I could have heard them first hand from him.

*   *   *

I always had a pretty good relationship with my daughter. When she was 11 or 12, suddenly our relationship went pretty much kaput -- where she was nasty and distant, withdrawn, surly -- and I couldn't figure out what was going on. I was expecting her to turn on us at 13 or 14. I wasn't expecting 11 or 12. But I remember at the soccer field, maybe a couple of months after this whole thing started, I kicked a ball at her and she kicked it back, and then I kicked it again and she kicked it back. So we're passing the ball back and forth. And I said, *Geez Honey, this is like old times. We're actually getting along.* And she says, *Dad, don't get used to it.* But I figured at least I had a little bit of a break through.

239

Almost as suddenly as the switch went off, it went back on and she was fine again. I remember it was a couple years after that. I asked her if she remembered that "bitch from hell" phase that she went through. She said, *Yeah, very much so.* I asked why she was acting like that. She said, *Because I thought I was supposed to.* She said all of her friends were complaining so much about their parents being this and that, that she thought that's what she was supposed to be doing.

*   *   *

I have a friend who was born in India. He's an IBM physicist. We've talked about how our kids don't appreciate what we've done and what they have. We live in a town where a lot of rich kids live. We would talk about how our kids are spoiled, and they just don't appreciate things like hard work and how you have to work in order to get things. We talked about sending our kids to India for a summer to get a better understanding of how blessed they are. We never did. Should have.

*   *   *

I would never ask my parents for a thing. They weren't poor, but didn't have much, and I was very reluctant to ask them for anything. My kids are less hesitant. But there are some other interesting things that have kicked in. Like, *Don't drive me to school in your Lexis. I don't want to be like the other kids.* A girl they know has two cars. She doesn't have a license yet but she has a hummer and a beamer. That's a real turnoff for my kids.

*   *   *

I tell my kids that the richest guy they know is probably this very quiet guy who lives next door. There's a book called "The Millionaire Next Door". That's him. He's a guy over 80 that's up on his roof with a leaf blower blowing out his own

240

gutters. But I think the guy is loaded from some conversations that he and I have had about the properties he owns, but no one would ever know it. He drives a '90 something station wagon. So I try to encourage my kids to think about real wealth versus just the ostentatious trappings they see in our town.

*　　*　　*

There are two fathers in our cul-de-sac. I look at them and I feel horrible for their children. The one guy's got three kids and the other guy's got two, and I just feel horrible. Why even bother? One's a sales guy and he's out partying every night. Never home. One of his daughters practically lives at our house. The other couple is just clueless. They just let their two kids go. I've never see the parents out of the house. The daughter is a really, really nice kid. She also lives at our house. And I say what a shame. It's just a shame. The one dad is actually home. I don't know what the hell he's doing, if he's playing around on his computer or whatever. He just couldn't care less. We always joke when he's out for "father-son day" once a year. He goes out and throws the ball around with his kid. And then he's yelling at him because he's not throwing the ball the right way. *What the hell are you doing? You got to crank it like this.* I'm thinking, what an idiot. You're out once a year. It's a joke. And when he's out there, he's critiquing the hell out of his son and telling him he's doing a shitty job in throwing the baseball. His son is 9 years old. He's really short but the dad thinks the kid is going to be this major league baseball player. And he wants him to play baseball because he played baseball. He wants him to play football because he never got to play football, and he wants him to play basketball. The kid doesn't have a shot at playing basketball. He doesn't have a shot at playing football. He's not a good baseball player either, and the father is out there drilling him on how to dip his shoulder with the bat. It's really a shame. All he does is yell at him.

*　　*　　*

I kept a journal for about 17 years. It wasn't a diary; it was a journal. Every once in a while, I would feel inspired to write something. And I had this strong desire to turn it into something to give to my children, which I did on my 50th birthday.

It took me about six months, and rather than arrange it chronologically, I did it topically. It included a letter to my two children saying why I was doing this. And then I wrote a sort of extensive handbook to it. One chapter was called "Fathers and Daughters." I wrote on things that had to do with my kids. One chapter was about death and one chapter was about banking. One chapter was about different careers I had. It had pictures. I gave it to them and family and friends. A lot of what I had in there were letters that I wrote to my kids. Also notes that I wrote to them, or conversations we'd had, or just reflections on them.

And then I wrote two books for my grandchildren. You know, children's books I had illustrated, and they thought that was neat. So in some ways I've learned more about being a father by being a grandfather because you're once removed. I've learned each kid is pretty different.

*　　*　　*

I started this little project. I'm recording interviews that my wife, our children and I conduct with my mother who's still alive, and with my wife's father who's still alive. You know, *What were we like when we were kids? How'd you raise us? What was your childhood like?*

As they reach my age, maybe even after I'm gone, wouldn't it be something neat for my kids to be able to have this and share it with their kids? To say I can reach back 100 years into my family life. I like that a lot.

*　　*　　*

My youngest daughter got out of college. We probably spent $100,000 on her education. Went to Ivy League school and she goes and decides to work at a Cheesecake Factory in Washington. I guess I could have said, *Nah*. I decided I was going to take an anthropological approach watching a kid coming out of college and transition into the adult world so to speak. And so rather than getting in her face or giving her direction or telling her this or telling her that, I thought it was going to work out. Things are going to work out.

So I sort of stepped back. I didn't get emotionally involved and I let her do her thing. My only concern was she had to take three tests for the Cheesecake Factory. She passed the first two and I knew the day she was taking the third. And I was on pins and needles. I said, *God forbid my daughter, the Brown graduate, doesn't pass the third test, which I think was on desserts.* And I'm sweating it like she's sitting for her medical boards or bar exam or something like that.

But I think there's a fine line between giving the impression you don't care and giving the impression that you're just letting them find themselves.

*   *   *

I had another instance where my daughter was teaching high school, which I thought was a great job. She decides she's going to quit. I wasn't particularly happy about that because I think teaching's a great profession. So she came over to see me. This is when I was in the career management business. I said to myself, whatever I say to her, I'll be on the losing side of it. If I say, *Stick with teaching*, she won't stick with it. I decided, she'll be fine. I mean she's not jumping off a cliff, and I've been without a job, so who am I to tell her not to do this? So anyway, she looks around. She does some interviewing. One day she comes over and she said, *You know what? I'm not made for an office job. I just got an offer* *from another high school and I'm going to take that. It pays $10,000 more.* And I said to myself, what a home run that was. I never put my nose in. I just listened to her; heard her out and she ended up doing, in my judgment, the right thing.

Did I do that when she was 8 or 10 or 12? Probably not, but you learn things. I think there's a fine line as to how much you direct. My wife is different; she gets more in their face. She doesn't think she does, but they read all the signals. They know exactly whether my wife liked what they bought or didn't buy, or what they were going to do or not do. But my view is as long as they're not going to do anything that I think is physically harmful or really stupid, my job is to just shut the hell up. If they ask for advice, I'll give them advice. But I have enough confidence that things will work out. They can try your soul or your patience. But so far, it's been fine.

*   *   *

I don't think religion has to be a key element in parenting, but it was important to my mom and she instilled that in me. It's incredibly important to my wife, and so she's instilled it in our kids. And I try to do so as well. Not by telling the kids, *You should be a strict Catholic.* But by teaching what the Catholic Church has meant to me and that the catechism tells us what we're supposed to do. It's *Know God, love God and serve God.* Part of being a good dad is following the example set by Jesus. He was a teacher. He was an authoritarian when He had to be. And He was an advisor and guide. He didn't shirk from what any good father would do. So the church can be a really good accessory to reinforce what a good father should do. This is my view. But I don't think it's essential. I mean if you're not Catholic or not religious, I don't think that prevents you from being a good dad. But it can help.

*   *   *

244

I became much more interested in religion after I got married and when my wife got pregnant. Now I'm much more religious than I ever was. When I first saw the sonogram of my son in 1996, it was a profound moment for me. In bringing back a fundamental belief in a higher power.

* * *

My wife and I went to Catholic grade school, high school and college. And my children went to Catholic grade school. My daughter's now in a Catholic high school. Religion is very important to us. The parish and the school have facilitated that dramatically. They played in CYO programs. They've done after school programs. It's very much a community in terms of the parish and the school and our being involved in a lot of different things. And the principal of the school has been there up until this year. She retired but is still involved and she did a great job. She focused on reminding the kids it was a Catholic school in the Catholic community. We're fortunate from that perspective.

* * *

They're good kids. We've had it easy. Our issues have been modest, but then you need to try to set the right framework for that so that you don't have problems later, or if you do, you have some framework to deal with them.

* * *

The bottom line is kids want to feel loved by their parents. And certainly fathers have a certain special place in the family, just as mothers do. But it's a different place. I just think it's important that the kids be able to connect with the father. You got to figure it out and it may change over time. In fact, I'm sure it will. There's probably stuff that I'm saying to my daughter and I don't even know how impactful it is for her right now. I'm sure it will come

245

back later when she's older and she can talk about it.

*   *   *

I feel blessed. I really do. My kids have some flaws around the edges. Nobody's perfect, but they're all basically very good people and good to each other, good to us.

*   *   *

Wordsworth said, *The child is the father of the man.* I think he was talking about your children helping you grow up and mature as an adult.

*   *   *

Some Additional Perspectives

Questions:

1   *What stories about your kids and family would you pass along to others?*

2   *What stories are your kids telling about you and how they were raised?*

3   *Is there any "conventional wisdom" that is holding you back from being a better dad?*

What You'd Do Differently

Maybe I would have spent more time at home instead of the office.

I could have spent more time with the kids.

Maybe I would baby the kids less.

Communicate more.

So, how do I think I'm doing as a father? I think I'm doing alright. I think I could be doing better. I spend time with the kids whenever I'm not working. And there are things I can participate in with them, which I do. They're both big into their karate so when I'm home, I drive them to karate school four times a week. But at the same time I don't think I have done enough. I think it's too late now. Things over the years to really encourage family, shared activities, bonding type of activities -- I feel like I'm missing all that. Part of that is my personality, quite frankly. But part of it is just not making the effort to do things.

*   *   *

What do normal families do together? You know, things like eating dinner together. We don't do that as much as we should. Trips? We take our vacations every year but I don't think that's enough. There's no lack of love in the family. That's not an issue for us, but I do think we lack some unity. We don't sit down and have easy conversations. It's rare.

*   *   *

I spend so much time working. And I don't think they really talk to their mother all that much. The kids and I, we actually have pretty good conversations in the car. That's when we're alone, the three of us. But as a family, I think we're missing out on something. Last week, we had dinner out. We actually had a nice time. The service was slow. Had a real conversation going about different things in school, like girls and dating, but it's rare that we do that.

And mom's not capable of connecting well with the kids, so everything falls to me. But I think we've done a good job raising good people. I know my daughter's already told me, *Dad, when I graduate high school, you're on your own. I'm not coming back. I love mom but I'm not coming back.* And I think the boy is going to be living with me forever. He's going to be 40 years old in the same room with a Grateful Dead t-shirt on, doing doobies with the door shut.

*   *   *

A mistake that I think I'm making is not spending as much time as I'd like to with my one daughter. My first daughter was a soccer player and a lacrosse player, and I played sports so we saw each other a lot in that context. I coached my son and I watched him play a ton of sports. With my older daughter at college, the constellation has changed from five to four. That means my wife spends time with my younger daughter and I'm doing more things

248

with my son. The mistake that I could be making is not creating more opportunities to switch. For me to take my daughter horseback riding, even when I don't know a damn thing about it. I need to break that natural pairing off. And it's not bad. I don't know whether she feels it or not. But I can see it.

*　　*　　*

Maybe I would baby the kids less. Maybe I should have instilled better study habits. But I think overall I'm doing okay. You have to decide what you need to do. I attend the big things at school and at games, but not everything. I could be doing more during the week, but my wife and I have made decisions about work and money and what is most important. I don't see regrets down the road.

*　　*　　*

I would probably instill more financial discipline in my kids. Let's say, spending comes very easy for them.

*　　*　　*

I think I pushed my first son a bit too much on sports. He was a great athlete. But he and my wife both say that my regret is exaggerated and that there's no problem. Still, I was easier on the other kids.

*　　*　　*

If I had it to do over again, I wish I was more sensitive during the time when my divorce occurred. I think kids take divorces really hard. What are the needs of the child? The family has decided to break up. What are all the transitional issues around having separate places to live and not having a room? I don't really have a room. When going through a divorce, you don't have a lot of money, so you can't have a big furnished apartment. You lose your private space, your sanctuary. There are times when I think I really failed as a dad. If we could look back, why did we break up?

*   *   *

Communicate more. Be more patient. Be less tough on the oldest one. I loosened up, but I wish I had figured it out earlier.

*   *   *

If I had to do it again, I would have our four kids right away. Not spread out over the twelve years that separates the oldest from the youngest. It was always hard to have family meals together. When my youngest was 6, the oldest was going off to college.

*   *   *

Maybe I would have spent more time at home instead of the office. But a lot of guys who I grew up with, now police and firemen, are still working two jobs to provide for their kids.

*   *   *

I remember the chance I had to take my son to a special sports event. I could have but didn't. I regret it.

*   *   *

In Europe apparently it's become acceptable, and in some cases from what I'm told, mandatory, to take a year off between high school and college. Some of the universities in Europe are mandating that you can't come right from high school. You got to go take a year off. I think I read a couple of schools in the states have begun this. They give suggestions like community service, travel, or project work. Get involved in something and do not just sit at home for a year.

So if I had it to do over again with my son, that's exactly what I would do. I would say, *Get a job for a year. Save up some money and I'll match it and it'll pay for some travel for a year.* Or maybe I would try to make arrangements for some work experience in a faraway place to give him some exposure. Make it a developmental year, a year of gaining maturity. Get out on his own. That would have been a great thing for him.

*   *   *

I could have spent more time with the kids, say by breaking away in the afternoon or spending more time having fun at the shore on weekends.

*   *   *

What You'd Do Differently

Questions:

1   *Looking back, are there any things you would do differently?*

2   *Do you feel trapped into thinking it's too late to make a change?*

3   *Are you capable of making the changes you wish to make? Is there any help you should seek?*

Advice

Be a man. Do what's right.

Being a father is for the rest of your life…. It's not a carefree life, so first make sure you're prepared.

Love them. Love them right now because "right now" passes very fast.

Don't be afraid of hard decisions.

You can't ever make up the time lost so don't ever try. Just don't lose it in the first place.

You have to show them love but you can't protect them from the real world. You have to prepare them for that.

I would say trust your instincts. I think the rare dad would be the one who just wings it; let's his kids do whatever the hell they want. I think with most dads, their instinctual desire would be to guide and be an influence or an authoritarian when you have to be. Just trust your gut. Most times, it will not be wrong. And don't be afraid to make a mistake. Kids are resilient. They're forgiving, especially when they're young. You're not going to break them. You're not going to ruin their lives by making a mistake. But you could ruin their lives by not being a father; not being what you think you need to be. We see evidence of that every day. Parents who didn't have the guidance and support of a father.

*   *   *

Let me give you one piece of advice. Somebody else gave me this and I have now lived it for the last four years. I lived in the same house for 26 years. It's a modest home. That's me. I'm not into that stuff. But somebody told me I might want to think about getting a second home in a place where my kids can come. So I did that. You know, a beach home. I tell you, I wouldn't have believed it but this has been the greatest thing I've done. And two weekends out of three, my kids are there. Usually we're there for most of those weekends and I've met all of their friends, all their significant others. We have dinner together. This weekend, my son has four guys coming down and two girls. We're going to be there. My kids are adults with their own lives and their own careers, and if I was just living at my main house they would never come. I wouldn't have believed it, but I did it and it's paid off.

*   *   *

Be available. Help your kids make good decisions. I don't think you can hurt anything if you advise them on decisions. Did I make decisions for them? I tried not to. We've been very careful with that. But my kids have each had relationships with people that I hoped would end. We really had to bite our tongues.

*   *   *

I don't think I missed a soccer game, a lacrosse game, or a basketball game. I can't remember what I missed. It's just a meeting on a calendar. I'd say to people at work, *I'm sorry, I have a meeting at that time.* Just do it. I can't imagine any employer, any boss, really cares as long as you're getting the job done. I think people think they care but in the end, they don't. You got to say, *Screw it.*

*　　*　　*

If I could only pass along one thing, I'd say, just have confidence in yourself and you'll make the right decisions. My boys have both expressed a little bit of a fear of fatherhood. They ask, *What if I do the wrong thing or I don't raise the kid right?* I tried to get them to put that aside. You're a good person. Don't expect too much. You're not going to raise a Nobel Laureate, don't expect it, don't try. You're not going to raise an all star sports hall of famer. Don't try to push them…don't live vicariously through your kids. I don't think I did, but I have come across parents who are doing that. Especially in sports.

*　　*　　*

The wife of a good buddy of mine is expecting in September. I just said to him, *Patrick. It's the biggest, most important thing you'll ever do in your life.*

*　　*　　*

I think your daughters marry their father. I read that on several occasions and I've seen it happen.

*　　*　　*

Just enjoy who they are, what they are. They literally go through different phases and I could remember that it's just amazing watching them learn when they were infants all the way up watching even now my 21 year old. She's still evolving from a young person to a young adult and that transition is just amazing. So try to enjoy every phase that they go through because it really is enjoyment.

*   *   *

My oldest kid. Did he kill anybody? No. Is he a drug abuser? No. Let him go through life. It's allowed me to be a little more subjective with my youngest. It's allowed me to say to myself that I've got to let her go through the learning curve herself. I know the right answer, but I also know that she's got to find it for herself. She is going to be a five year student because of this and that and the other thing. It's irritating to us, but by the same token I know that she's got to go through that herself. She's changed her mind three times on what she wants to do, and she still doesn't know.

*   *   *

None of my kids has the success ambition that I have. As a matter of fact, I think they would all say, and one actually has said to me, they consciously rejected my lifestyle. I think I'm a workaholic. I work a lot of hours. I travel an awful lot and that's just not for them. If that's what success means, they are going to try it differently. They reject it. All three of them actually rejected the colleges that we hoped they would consider. They didn't want to hear anything about it. They want their own deal. The one thing I do encourage them to do is treat life as an adventure. You get to lead your way. Now there's an assumption there that you're going to be productive and you're not going to harm people. You don't get to be a mass murderer. Life is an adventure and take full advantage of it.

But your adventure is different from my adventure. Find

things that you'll love to do and that you're passionate about and that's the way to enjoy life. For each of them it's different but I think they're doing that. In that sense I guess they're following in my footsteps because I look at my life and I think I've had a pretty good adventure, and I don't think it's over yet.

*   *   *

Be a man. Do what's right.

*   *   *

The first thing I would say is, *Be responsible.* Being a father is for the rest of your life so you've got to be prepared for many years of shelter, food, and clothing. It's not a carefree life, so first let's make sure you're prepared. But beyond that, enjoy the hell out of it, really love them, participate with them in as much of their lives as you possibly can.

*   *   *

Be yourself.

*   *   *

If you have challenges and problems, don't take care of them alone. You probably aren't going to run into anything that somebody else hasn't run into. Don't be afraid to ask. Women are better at this than men. Women will chat with each other about the challenges they are having with the kids. Men should just talk about it every once in a while with friends or family.

*   *   *

My wife and I never really talked about how we wanted to raise the kids. I was very different from what she was. I have

256

different inclinations, different styles, tactics and so forth. We would have benefited from that.

*　　　*　　　*

Play with the kids. Work hard but when you're not at work try to be present. Take a hard line when it's needed but when it's time to check out, check out.

*　　　*　　　*

Drawing a hard line is one piece of advice. I wouldn't baby kids. I'm not saying you hit them, but you really got to be like my father was. Don't be afraid of hard decisions.

*　　　*　　　*

I think relaxing a little is a good thing. Not worrying so much. It's so hard. You need to worry about kids all the time these days and I mean that in multiple. But are they going to wind up robbing gas stations if they're not in 15 activities during the day? When we were kids, we just went out and played. I think a little unstructured social time is very good. So don't always structure their social calendars.

*　　　*　　　*

I do think it's important to be very friendly with them. I don't get the hard line. I don't want my kids to be afraid of me. I think having fun with them is important. My brother-in-law, who I really admire, will go out and play Capture the Flag with the kids for two hours. That's what my father used to do and I loved that. I'll do it on our vacation. We play wiffle ball for hours and hours. Play with them. Don't go watch them play.

*　　　*　　　*

One other thing I find personally very rewarding is teaching and playing games with them like Cribbage and Gin Rummy. We haven't taken to chess but we play checkers. Those kinds of games are great. I play video games with the kids. There are a lot of them. We don't discourage it. We go play with them. My wife will be with them when I get home from work. She's playing Wii with the kids. Kicking her leg up bowling.

*   *   *

Two things. One is spend time. There's no time spent with them that you'll ever regret. Spend time with them and be supportive. The second thing is tap into their passion. That passion certainly can change over time. If I look back, my passion has changed from the time I was a kid to a teenager to a young adult to a married adult. Try and help them tap into their passion. It's amazing. I'll see my kids light up when they're doing something they really like.

*   *   *

Time is love. I think it's really important to understand it's all about them. It's not about us as dads. As they get older and things come up, be really good at listening and understanding what their issues are and what they're really trying to say rather than focusing on your own stuff. Be open and really get to a level of communication where anything can be said even though your feelings might be hurt.

*   *   *

I think it's important to have fun and play together. I think it's also important to cry together too. Be able to shed a tear. Could be a 68 on a chemistry test. Could be a loss of a friend. When a relationship breaks up. Be available. It's the same qualities that make it work in business, too. Being available, being responsive,

258

being there.

*   *   *

A CEO told me this. He said, *As soon as you see a problem, it's not going to get better without a change. Make the change.* That would be good advice for parents. You can't over-react. It became clear for us.

*   *   *

I'm trying to figure if there's a model for relationships growing up. We come into the world and we're totally dependent. You need your diapers changed. And then the next phase is counter dependent. *Everything you say I'm going to disagree with.* And then the next phase would be independent where, *I'm off on my own. Don't bother me. I just need to break away from the family.* And then the ideal phase is when you get to a point of interdependency. You recognize that, *I've got some good stuff, and I recognize what you know, so let's put our heads together.* That's where I think my son and I finally got to. He's doing great now. He's found his niche and he's happy. He's got great friends. Every now and then he has a financial problem, and if he needs help, I help him. So, getting to that interdependent phase and not getting hung up on the counter dependent phase where you say black, I say white. Where everything is argumentative. It's the recognition that a child growing up is seeking his or her own identity. I'm not a psychologist but that's why some kids wind up with all kinds of body piercing and purple hair.

*   *   *

I don't think I have any pithy advice other than enjoy it. I'm surprised at how fast it goes, how fast each stage goes. My older son went through these stages where his first was the Peter Pan stage. We watched the Peter Pan movie, must have been one hundred times. Everything in life was about Peter Pan. Then we

259

went through the Toy Story phase and we watched that thing over and over and over again. It's baseball right now. We sit and watch baseball. We watched the All Star game. We went to Cooperstown a couple of weeks ago for vacation. But it's all baseball all the time and it's to the point where I'm sick of talking about baseball, but I know that will pass. If I missed the Peter Pan stage, or the Toy Story stage, I don't get it back. And I don't know what the next stages are but I will try to connect and embrace them.

*   *   *

Love them. Love them right now because "right now" passes very fast.

*   *   *

I don't know that I am the best person to ask for advice. Other than it's a daunting task. A couple things though. You can't ever make up the time lost so don't ever try. Just don't lose it in the first place. If you ever feel that you have to make up for lost time, then you already lost the opportunity. They just don't come back. No rewind.

Number two, whatever the right word is, nurture. You have to create an environment where they can learn from their mistakes. You have to give them enough room to make mistakes. I've seen too many younger parents try to prevent exposure to anything that could be risky. If you don't have some risks, if you don't learn to take risks, you don't learn to recover. I see that in a lot of different dimensions where people try to create too much of a perfect world. They think that if they give their children a perfect world, they'll become perfect children, which is fruitless.

And then third, spend more time listening than talking. There's always time to talk but it's very hard to listen. The child needs to talk more than to listen. The parent needs to listen

260

although they're predisposed to doing the talking. If you can do those three things, you probably will be largely successful.

*　　*　　*

The best consultant is going to ask questions and then shut up because you learn more from listening than you do from talking. The same rule applies to parenting. If you're a good listener, the kids will tell you more than you want to know if you afford them the opportunities. And the more you give them the opportunity, the more they'll learn from what they're discussing with you, as opposed to if you just tell them, *These are my rules.*

*　　*　　*

Fathers are a role model for their kids. My advice to fathers would be recognize the truth of that and then ask, *Okay. If I'm going to be a role model, whether I like it or not, then what sort of person do I want them to follow, and what do I want them to be?* And then be that person. Avoid doing anything wrong because they will learn from you both the good and the bad. They take on the bad and they repeat it. If you don't want that, then you can't do the bad. I know the English here is shocking but you see what I mean. You can't do something wrong and then turn around to your kids and say, *But <u>you</u> shouldn't do this.* That's a load of crap. I mean you can't do that. Never underestimate how smart your kids are. Whether it's an actual intellectual level or whether it is an emotional intelligence. They absorb everything and they learn so much from you. So recognize that fact and modify your behavior.

*　　*　　*

To me there's no excuse. I had a violent, alcoholic father and I was a parent at a very young age and I had all of that financial pressure and everything else. Well, okay. I can make myself a victim of that or I can step out and say, *Okay, some of this*

261

is my decision. Some of it isn't. Where it's your decision, make the right decisions as best you can. Where it's not your decision, recognize that it's not your fault. I actually have little tolerance for people that use excuses unless it's something really dramatic like sexual assault or something along those lines. Suppose you've had a tough relationship with your parents. Don't turn that into an excuse for perpetuating that with your own relationships. Be stronger. Recognize that your kids are going to follow what you do.

*   *   *

Kids need encouragement and maybe a little push now and then. But there is a fine line beyond which you can push too much. You can turn them off. And you can signal that they can never please you.

*   *   *

There's nothing wrong with being a bit analytical about it. Make a list. Look around you. Don't be afraid to look around for best practices. In a way, that's what we did by looking at our two upbringings and selecting the best practices. The other thing is you have to show them love but you can't protect them from the real world. You have to prepare them for that. That's the major part of your responsibility. The best way to do that is to openly talk to them about the challenges that you faced. When we had to cut back on our spending at home, we talked to the kids about it. Your kids are part of the process. We asked, *What are you going to sacrifice?* And they would say, *Okay, well, I can do without this and I can do without that.*

*   *   *

Find the time. Whether it's meal time or football or whatever it is. But find time to have family time. That dinner time discussion. Commit to being a family.

*   *   *

I get along really well with my kids, and I was very close to my kids, but I never want to be one of these parents that had to be their best friend as well. I am their best friend, but I'm the parent first. I've met some of the parents that would go night clubbing with their kids. I'd rather eat my own arm than going night clubbing with my kids. I mean, *Hello*. Now I'll go to the pub with them and have a drink. We go out to dinner. Of course we do all that sort of stuff, but would I go out night clubbing? Not a chance in hell. Would I go to a party with them? No. Not unless it's with the family. Why? Because you have to be the parent. And that means saying *No* sometimes. It's tougher for a best friend to do that. I think it's easier for a parent to do it, although I see a lot of parents shrink from that role of being a parent. I've been out and been drunk with my kids, but I was always the parent at the end of the day. If you don't put parenting first, the roles will clash when you draw the line because you confuse your kids.

*   *   *

You have to say *No*. We've often said to our kids, *Just get with the program. You may not like it but that's the way it is.*

*   *   *

There has to be a point of differentiation. They need that generational difference because it tells them that it's okay to start being your own person. You don't have to like everything your parents do. And that's fine because they're old and out of date.

*   *   *

Don't expect your kids to be better than you. If I really

263

don't want my kids to smoke and drink and drive, but I smoke and I drink and drive? Or I don't want them to abuse other people but I abuse other people? My son likes to bust my chops when I'm driving like a crazy man or when I correct him for something. He says, *I learned it by watching you*, and that's true. They do learn it by watching you. So if you give them a model, a good example, and they don't follow it, you have a right to challenge them or criticize them or force the issue with them. Don't try, *I made some mistakes but I had a reason that I made these mistakes and you don't have the same reasons so you're not allowed to make these mistakes*. That's not going to carry any weight. Your story has to be believable and supportable every step of the way, and you can't cop out by saying, *Well, my father wasn't as good as your father is, so it's okay that I'm whatever*. It doesn't mean you have to be perfect but you have to be honest and you have to be accountable for your own actions if you expect your kids to be accountable.

*   *   *

We've never asked any of them to do anything that we wouldn't do ourselves or to be anything that we didn't think they're capable of being. We haven't unfairly pushed anybody. Could my son have been a doctor if I pushed him? Probably, but he didn't have the desire. We had a neighbor that took the two older ones down to see knee replacement surgery one time in the summer when they were off. She came home saying, *Yuck. Never in a million years*. He came home saying, *That's cool. I think I might want to do that*. You got to have a passion to invest that many years in school and that much effort in something. If you don't have the passion it's never going to work out. So we've never really pushed them. We certainly have high expectations. They know it. They know we're proud of them. We certainly have always reinforced things they've done well and the things they've done to make us proud.

*   *   *

Listen to your kids. No request is too insignificant, but don't give them everything they want. Make them earn half of what they get.

*   *   *

Give them responsibility early and often and let their decisions be their decisions. My kids would probably tell you they got so sick of hearing their father say, *Don't ever come home and tell me you followed Johnny off the cliff. Tell me you organized the revolution in the school and they followed you off the cliff. I'll respect you more. It'll still be bullshit, but I will respect you more.* That one they heard early and often. Don't come home and tell me you did it because everybody did. I don't respect that.

*   *   *

My experience as a recruiter says to me that the relationship with one's father has a great deal to do with the person's success in life. I interview so many people and I'm always fascinated by it. I'm fascinated by birth order. I'm fascinated by relationship with parents. I think that it's recognizable when a successful guy or a girl has a great relationship with their dad. I actually think, and this is not to dismiss the importance of a mom obviously, but a father will have a critical impact on the way a child feels about him or herself. I think it's a great predictor of future success. If we did a study, I think I could prove it. Is this advice for a new father? Yes. I would say, be mindful of that. A big part of your child's confidence will come through the relationship that you have with your child.

*   *   *

It's hard being a kid. Leave them alone. Be loving. Be supportive. And I really think that pays huge dividends. It did for me. I'm very lucky because of what's going on with my kids. What

265

they've done in life I'm proud of, but it's more. It's a really nice relationship. It's something that I would wish for anybody else. You have to really suck it up and make compromises yourself as a parent in order to give that child that feeling. Screw around with them. Have fun with them. I always believed in showing them outrageous behavior.

This was a really funny story. My son was in high school. I guess a sophomore. We went to Wawa together and in the parking lot were these kids who were from his school that he recognized. They were wearing the jeans real low and their boxer shorts hanging out. Skateboarding types of cool guys. And my son didn't want to get out of the car; didn't want to be embarrassed. Maybe because he was with his dad. And in response to that, I parked the car in a place where they could see me. I got out of the car and I unbuckled my pants and I lowered them down to expose my underwear and I went out and engaged these kids. *Hey. How you guys doing?* And my son was just horrified. He was dying from it. It was like the worst thing that happened to him. I hope that I was showing him that none of this crap matters. It's just stupid. Embarrassing my kid and having fun and showing him that most of this stuff is just bullshit, I think, was always part of his education.

*   *   *

Stay connected. Be alert. Understand what they are doing. Don't be naïve. Be on the lookout for drinking and drugs. When they show up, deal with it. Don't duck it. Be supportive and give advice, but there will be times you need to step in as the disciplinarian.

*   *   *

Take your kids' side 100% of the time. They'll know you do 100% of the time, and if they get 5 out of 100 over on you, fine. I don't make any decision in my life that's 95% right. That's better than I do day by day. So I'm going to err on that side and I think that they'll grow up with a sense of confidence in themselves. Just talk to them like people. Don't treat them like babies. They're smart. They have an opinion. Let them know you want to hear their opinion. Listen to them. Listen to what they say. Sometimes great insight comes out of young mouths. So listen to it. I think it's pretty cool for a kid when they make some argument and you say, *You got that one right. I'm with you on that one. I'm going with you.* In other words, *I'm betting on you.* My kids always know I'm betting on them. I'm investing. If they were stock, I'm buying. *Whatever you got I'm buying. I'll buy every share.*

*   *   *

Don't get mad over stupid things. At a minimum, it's worthless. It doesn't help, and worst case, it separates you from your kid. That builds a wall between you and your child. You have to remember that kids, particularly teenagers, by nature are liars. They don't tell the truth because they want to avoid getting in trouble. So stick with the real priorities and stay focused and don't be thrown by the little stuff; the getting in trouble here and there and the note from the teacher. You know, fuck that. Who cares? Most of the teachers who I see are imbeciles anyway. I was fine with most of my teachers. I just always had a healthy disregard for them. I got that from my parents actually, and my parents are both teachers.

*   *   *

Number one, definitely accept and celebrate each of their individualities so that they know that they have their own strengths and challenges and weaknesses. You need to say, *I'm proud of you.* Be responsible. Be good to their mother. Be available. Make sure they know that you're always there to listen to them and to share with them. Go out of your way when it is inconvenient. Most times it is tough to put on that face when you come home. But know that

267

soon, they'll be at college. Their time is going to be their time. Whereas right now you can choose everyday to spend as much time as you want with your children because soon enough they're going to say, *Dad, I just don't want to hang out with you right now. I want to hang out with my friends. Just not cool anymore.* You only have a short time to spend some time with them; to have some fun with them and just be there for them. I know it's kind of cliché but it's genuine.

*   *   *

I'm very huggy, kissy. That's how my dad is. When he walks in, he gives me a kiss on the lips. My boys, I'm like that with them every single day. Recently, my oldest, he knows it's coming. So he'll say, *Dad, please don't kiss me when I get home.* He's only 8. The youngest is still very touchy, feely, huggy, kissy and we as a family are like that. A good friend of mine told me that his dad never even looked at him let alone hugged or kissed him or said *Hi* to him or *I love you.* He said he really learned from me, and now I see him with his son. He kisses him and he hugs him. Some guys say, *I don't give hugs to my son. That's too much physical contact. That's too much. I'm babying them.* No. No way.

*   *   *

Get involved with your kids' lives. Help them get a good start. Be there. Show up. Ask questions and listen. Also, be human. Admit when you make mistakes. And ensure a strong relationship with your wife. When later in life my kids are forming their own relationships, I want them to look back at their parents for a model of what a good relationship is.

*   *   *

Pay attention to your kids. Love them. Be there for them. Be available for them. Find out what they like, and do that with them.

268

*   *   *

If you are going to be a father, it will take a lot of time. More than you think. Involvement is huge as a parent. It shouldn't be quiet involvement. Kids need you to be there. But you don't want to live vicariously through your kids and use them to feed your own ego. Today a lot of parents are missing from their kids' games because of their own work and social schedules. What a shame. Kids take time, money and a full-person commitment.

*   *   *

As a coach, it's okay for your players to hurt when they lose. That helps them learn commitment. But you do not want them to be devastated from a loss – you want them to learn from it. Same with your kids.

*   *   *

There is no perfect definition of good parenting. Don't try to be perfect. But be involved. Your kids should know that you have sacrificed for them. You can't buy their development – except with your own time and involvement.

*   *   *

Forge relationships based on respect. It's okay to have your own point of view. But listen to them, ask a lot of questions, and get to the core of their issues. Carve out time for each of your kids. Let them talk, or not. Spending time with them doesn't have to be complicated - - take them with you to the cleaners.

*   *   *

Spend time with your kids. Don't outsource parenthood. Postpone material things to spend time with them now. Now is when they need you. The more time you spend with them, the better you can understand them, and influence them. I don't mean control them, but help shape them.

*   *   *

Don't hesitate to say, *Look. Give me a minute here. This is the first time I ever raised a 20 year old.*

*   *   *

You always need to be there, and because you want to be there, not because you're obligated to be there. You really want to be a part of every aspect of your kids' lives while they're growing up, and hopefully I met that standard pretty well, even working in the career that I had at the time which was very time consuming. I coached all my kids in all the sports whether it was busy season or non-busy season. I have three children and I didn't miss a kid or miss a season. I found the time. It was never a problem to find the time. I always wanted to do those things.

*   *   *

Love your kids no matter what. Teach them, guide them, discipline them and love them no matter what. There can't be any condition. Unfortunately, our actions too often involve withdrawal of love as a way of teaching them. It's not necessarily a punishment to people but it's a way of teaching. *I'm mad at you. I don't want to talk to you.* That doesn't work. Keep talking to them and keep loving them. More than keep talking to them, you have to keep loving them.

*   *   *

One of the biggest challenges for any parent came actually from Irma Bombeck, a columnist who wrote on families years ago.

She said one of the biggest challenges that a parent faces is figuring out what age-appropriate freedom is. At any age, whether it's 10, 12, 15 or 18 or 21, how do you build the sense of managing freedom and being free within the confines of what's possible or advisable at a certain age? Certainly, what you allow a 10 year old to do is very different than you allow a 14 year old to do. But you better be moving along the scale a little bit to allow different freedoms for different ages as they grow up. But trying to figure out what those are and how to give kids a chance to reach but not exceed their grasp is a very difficult process, but one you have to keep working at. The biggest challenge is to try to figure things out along the way. And as you figure them out, don't be satisfied that you've figured them out because the situation will change, the kid will change, and the age of freedom will change. You need to constantly be trying to evaluate what's working or what's not working and be willing to change.

*　　*　　*

No matter how fast it goes by, you can't capture it. That's where I'm lucky, incredibly lucky. That's the biggest learning. Watching my daughter grow up. She was born one day, the next day she graduated from college. You know the drill. I can't say that I haven't missed a moment with my younger ones, but I don't miss many. As part of my new career, I'm now home so much more with them rather than working 70 hours a week. I have boundaries. I don't miss recitals, baseball games, basketball games.

*　　*　　*

You owe your kids a good start in life. A good education. I'm still paying for loans, but I don't have a single regret.

*　　*　　*

271

Find out what your kids like and do that with them, with other people you like and respect. Listen to them. Learn what they are passionate about.

*   *   *

Teach your kids to be team players, to never quit, to honor commitments, and to adapt to new situations. Ask yourself: *How can I help them? How can I help them rise to new challenges?*

*   *   *

You need to spend time with them because it's fun but also because you want it to be a learning experience. Every parent is tired, stretched and stressed. But you need to dig deeper because you are responsible for giving them a start in life...and a start in how to become a good parent themselves.

*   *   *

It's okay to fail. J.K. Rowling has a great speech about the importance of failing, and I think it's important to teach kids about failing. You know, and picking themselves up and getting back on the bicycle or getting back on the math test or whatever the hell it is. How you fail and how you recover is more important than how you win. And a lot of kids, I fear today while I'm standing on sidelines and listening to parents, are not being taught that. So your kid fails a test. *Okay. Take a look at it and understand what you got wrong. You understand why? Was it sloppy? Was it sloppy thinking? Or was it something conceptually you didn't understand?* Taking them through that is a very important thing to learn.

*   *   *

It's amazing what kids will believe from their parents.

You're a role model. I think that that was one of the very good things about both my parents. They both had very different styles but from the standpoint of being very good role models, they were excellent. I never saw either one of my parents abuse alcohol. Yeah, my dad smoked for a while, but actually my brother and I kicked him of that habit by playing tricks on him with his cigarette packs. But you've got a lot of influence over your kids. You got to use it correctly and wisely.

*   *   *

The other thing that I have found to be effective with my kids in terms of getting through to them is - - I never saw this with my parents - - being totally goofy and irreverent with them. That just shows a side of dad which they don't see so much with mom. Unfortunately, she's got a ton of things on her plate and has to deal with them. But I think that it's important for them to see a lighter side of you. They'll understand that you're a real person. And there are things I do today that are things that I would have been doing as a kid. I enjoy doing it and I might as well let the kids see it. And they see that spontaneous joy from dad and they're like, *Oh that's interesting*, though sometimes they might get embarrassed by it.

*   *   *

My father, even though he wasn't outwardly as animated as my mother, was a very emotional guy. I saw that and it was okay. It was okay for him. Being Italian, this may be a little different than, say, a German family and I've seen that contrast between my family and my wife's family. It's not that one's right and one's wrong. It's just different. But I do think it is important to show emotions with your kids at the appropriate time because that's real.

*   *   *

You can't say *Yes* all the time. But help them understand

273

why *No* is the right answer. Even when they are young.

*   *   *

I think one of the trickier things for any parent, and certainly the father, is, as your kids get older, how much independence do you give them? And unfortunately there's no hard and fast rule about that. I just think you got to be continually thinking about that. And you have to understand that things are going to happen to your kids that are not pleasant, either because of the choices they make or choices other people make directed towards them. And you can't protect them from everything that's unpleasant. Kids need to experience failure and difficulty, and as you give them more independence, that's going to happen.

It will be interesting to see if this comes to pass with my kids but I've seen it with my siblings and my wife's siblings. You see a person making bad choices. Some people have the attitude that they're going to adopt that person as their project and save them from themselves. And I hate to say it but think about your own kids. When they get to a certain age, you can't direct them anymore. They're going to be on their own and they're going to make some mistakes that are going to hurt you dearly. But you can't stop it. I think all you can do is be as supportive as you can and be there for them, but you're not going to be able to change them and that's a difficult thing to deal with. It really is.

*   *   *

My parents, as much as I love them dearly, and as much as they had a lot of the same values in common, were not on the same page. I would see them argue and it used to kill me. I thought I could be the peacemaker. I guess when I was about 21 years old I finally realized this is like knocking my head against the wall. And I eventually said to them, *You know what? Don't look to me to help you out. This is your problem, you guys figure it out. I can't help you.*

274

This applies to your kids, too. At some point, while they're still your kids and you care about them, some kids are going to make some bad choices. Hopefully they are not life threatening. If you can impress upon them that they should make changes, then that's what you should try to do. But you cannot make them change. I've seen people try to get somebody to change, but at the end of the day, there's just a limit to what you can do. I've seen an awful lot of people get really frustrated and depressed over the fact that they can't save somebody from themselves. I think you have to understand there's a limit to what you can do with another human being. And I think it's especially difficult with your own child. My guess is, I'm going to see that with my kids. Hopefully it won't be that serious.

*   *   *

My wife and I have some issues around exactly how much can we can affect the kids at this age. How much can you control? When is there a law of diminishing returns? When everything you try continues to blow up, when are you doing more harm than good? That versus just giving up and not trying.

*   *   *

You're going to have enormous influence over your kids. Recognize that. Decide who the person is that you want to become and that you want your kids to see. Not in a dishonest way. But think consciously about what that person looks like. And then become that person.

*   *   *

275

Advice

Questions:

1 *Does any of this advice make sense to you? Is there some you disagree with?*

2 *Is there any advice you want to adopt? How will you do so? When?*

3 *What is missing? What are these dads not saying that you believe is important?*

4 *What three pieces of advice would you offer other dads who are just starting out? Who have young kids? Who have teenagers? Who have older kids?*

Afterword

Fatherhood: In Pieces. Double meaning? Besides conveying bite-size pieces of fatherly advice, does the title suggest that fatherhood, as an institution, is "in pieces?" As in attacked, devalued, debunked, ripped up, written off, or thrown away?

Well, yes. Sadly, our popular culture marginalizes fathers. We are depicted as dumb, dopey and out of touch. We are shown to be violent and abusive more often than noble and caring. Our role has been outsourced to the government, blithely combined into the dual role of a single mother, or simply discarded as obsolete.

Some of this, no doubt, derives from a number of social agendas whose aims include tossing traditional fatherhood on some 21st century trash heap. Some, though, is self-inflicted, with too many guys doing a lousy job taking care of their kids. Guys whose immaturity, stupidity, selfishness, or laziness prevents them from bringing to the table the love, caring, hard work, and sacrifice that being a father requires. To these guys I offer a piece of advice: Don't have kids. Period.

But for those who think they are ready, know this: it's hard work, it's for a life-time, and it will change your life profoundly. Bringing another life into the world is serious business. So, as one of these fathers said, "Be a man. Do the right thing." And experience a thrill unlike anything else in this world.

And while you're being a good dad, you'll be showing the world why, now more than ever, fatherhood is so critically important. We need good fathers. We need their courage and strength, their good humor and hard work, their protection, judgment, perseverance, discipline and love. Fathers who, along with loving mothers, offer the best chance for that newborn -- and our families, communities and country -- to grow and thrive.

277

Appendix

Make a list. Now it's your turn. Write down ten "keepers," suggestions from this book that you want to adopt and make your own. Talk with your spouse about them. They could be pieces of advice you never thought of, or they could be confirmations of what you already believe and routinely practice. But write them down. Look at the list on a regular basis, even daily. Figure out how you will make them part of your life today, this week, during your next family dinner, or on your next vacation. What do you need to start doing, stop doing, or continue doing? Don't wait. Start now.

Ten, Twenty or Thirty. If you want to do something or become something – like an entrepreneur, a doctor, an artist, a nurse, a builder, a designer, an engineer, a sales executive, a Marine, or a good father – go and talk with a number of people in that role. Make a discussion outline. Ask questions. Find out what makes them proud. Discover where the pitfalls are. Ask what they'd do differently? Ask for advice. Listen. Take notes. Synthesize. Form takeaways. Decide what you need to do to accomplish what you want to accomplish or become what you want to become. And then start doing it!

Divorce and "Modern Families." One friend's reaction to the manuscript of this book was along the lines of, *Sounds like most of the guys you interviewed have stable marriages. Some of their wives work in the home. It's a lot easier for them raising kids. They didn't face the problems that divorcees and single parents face.* Another asked, *What about the lousy economy and high unemployment? What can a father realistically do when he doesn't have a job? What do you say to them?*

I spoke with happily married guys and divorced guys. I'd say, and they would agree, that raising kids can be difficult for any family or parental structure. That two parents in a stable marriage makes it "easier" is probably why this structure has been preferred by all societies for thousands of years. Something tells me we should think twice before buying into the ideas of some folks who say that married fathers and mothers are obsolete. But whatever structure you're in, the responsibilities you have as a father are still yours. Each kid has one biological father. If each kid needs a provider, protector, disciplinarian, coach, and the other roles depicted in this book, then your question becomes, *How will I fulfill my responsibilities **regardless** of family structure?*

A shortage of jobs? Sure, this is tough, but this challenge is not unique to today. Guys have forever worked two and three jobs to put food on the table and a roof over their kids' heads. They're *your* kids and *your* responsibility. Sorry, but economic hardships don't change that.

To all fathers, regardless of your circumstances, I humbly offer three pieces of advice: Put your kids' needs and happiness before your own. Put your role of father before your other roles. And then bust your butt doing the very best you can.

Good luck to all of you.

Bill

About the Author

For more than thirty years, Bill McCusker has worked in the business world where he has held leadership roles, often with global responsibility, in large professional services firms. He and his wife, Tracye, taught school as U.S. Peace Corps volunteers on an outer island in Fiji for three years. Bill received a BA from the University of Notre Dame and an MBA from the University of Michigan. He was born and raised in New Jersey where he still lives with his wife and their two daughters, Kelly and Mary.